RENEWING
YOUR MIND

VICTORY SERIES

STUDY 4

RENEWING
YOUR MIND

BECOME MORE LIKE CHRIST

NEIL T. ANDERSON

BETHANY HOUSE
a division of Baker Publishing Group
www.BethanyHouse.com

© 2014 by Neil T. Anderson

Published by Bethany House Publishers
11400 Hampshire Avenue South
Bloomington, Minnesota 55438
www.bethanyhouse.com

Bethany House Publishers is a division of
Baker Publishing Group, Grand Rapids, Michigan

Printed in the United States of America

Library of Congress Cataloging-in-Publication Data is on file at the Library of Congress, Washington, DC.

ISBN 978-0-7642-1372-4

Cover design by Inside Out Design

14 15 16 17 18 19 20   7 6 5 4 3 2 1

Contents

Introduction   7

Session One: Being Transformed

1. Renewing Our Minds (Romans 12:1–8)   13

2. Tearing Down Mental Strongholds (2 Corinthians 10:1–5)   17

3. Letting Christ Rule in Our Hearts (Psalm 119:1–16)   21

4. Choosing the Truth (Philippians 4:4–9)   25

5. Observing God's Word (Ezra 7:8–10)   29

Session Two: Living Under Grace

1. Dead to Sin (Romans 6:1–14)   37

2. The Christian's Relationship to the Law (Mark 2:23–28)   41

3. Walking with God (Matthew 11:28–30)   45

4. Led by the Spirit (Exodus 13:17–22)   49

5. Enduring Hardship (Hebrews 12:1–13)   53

Session Three: Overcoming Anger

1. Emotional Honesty (1 Samuel 18:1–16)   61

2. A Humble Walk With God (Micah 6:6–8)   65

3. Goals and Desires (Luke 12:13–21)   69

Contents

4. A True Sense of Worth (2 Peter 1:3–11) 73

5. Righteous Indignation (Mark 11:12–25) 77

Session Four: Overcoming Anxiety

1. Dealing With Worry (Matthew 6:19–34) 85

2. Double-Minded Thinking (Joshua 24:14–28) 89

3. "Plan A" Living (Mark 7:1–9) 93

4. Knowing God's Ways (Jeremiah 9:1–26) 97

5. Casting Our Anxieties on Christ (1 Peter 5:6–10) 101

Session Five: Overcoming Depression

1. Diagnosing Depression (Psalm 38:1–22) 109

2. The Basis for Our Hope (Psalm 13:1–6) 113

3. Overcoming Hopelessness (Hebrews 6:13–19) 117

4. The Problem of Helplessness (Exodus 6:6–12) 121

5. Overcoming Helplessness (Numbers 13:26–14:9) 125

Session Six: Overcoming Losses

1. Reacting to Losses (Mark 10:32–34) 135

2. Surviving the Crisis (Job 3:1–26) 139

3. Identifying Losses (Acts 9:1–31) 143

4. The Elijah Complex (1 Kings 19:1–18) 147

5. Commitment to Overcome Depression (John 5:1–18) 151

Leader's Tips 157

Notes 161

Victory Series Scope and Sequence Overview 163

Books and Resources 167

Index 171

Introduction

The Victory Series

S o then, just as you received Christ Jesus as Lord, continue to live in him, rooted and built up in him, strengthened in the faith as you were taught" (Colossians 2:6–7). Paul's New Covenant theology is based on who we are "in Christ." As a believer in Christ, you must first be rooted "in Him" so you can be built up "in Him." Just as you encounter challenges as you grow physically, you will encounter hurdles as you grow spiritually. The following chart illustrates what obstacles you need to overcome and lessons you need to learn at various stages of growth spiritually, rationally, emotionally, volitionally, and relationally.

Levels of Conflict

	Level One Rooted in Christ	Level Two Built up in Christ	Level Three Living in Christ
Spiritual	Lack of salvation or assurance (Eph. 2:1–3)	Living according to the flesh (Gal. 5:19–21)	Insensitive to the Spirit's leading (Heb. 5:11–14)
Rational	Pride and ignorance (1 Cor. 8:1)	Wrong belief or philosophy (Col. 2:8)	Lack of knowledge (Hos. 4:6)
Emotional	Fearful, guilty, and shameful (Matt. 10:26–33; Rom. 3:23)	Angry, anxious, and depressed (Eph. 4:31; 1 Pet. 5:7; 2 Cor. 4:1–18)	Discouraged and sorrowful (Gal. 6:9)

	Level One Rooted in Christ	Level Two Built up in Christ	Level Three Living in Christ
Volitional	Rebellious (1 Tim. 1:9)	Lack of self-control (1 Cor. 3:1–3)	Undisciplined (2 Thess. 3:7, 11)
Relational	Rejected and unloved (1 Pet. 2:4)	Bitter and unforgiving (Col. 3:13)	Selfish (1 Cor. 10:24; Phil. 2:1–5)

This VICTORY SERIES will address these obstacles and hurdles and help you understand what it means to be firmly rooted in Christ, grow in Christ, live free in Christ, and overcome in Christ. The goal of the course is to help you attain greater levels of spiritual growth, as the following diagram illustrates:

Levels of Growth

	Level One Rooted in Christ	Level Two Built up in Christ	Level Three Living in Christ
Spiritual	Child of God (Rom. 8:16)	Lives according to the Spirit (Gal. 5:22–23)	Led by the Spirit (Rom. 8:14)
Rational	Knows the truth (John 8:32)	Correctly uses the Bible (2 Tim. 2:15)	Adequate and equipped (2 Tim. 3:16–17)
Emotional	Free (Gal. 5:1)	Joyful, peaceful, and patient (Gal. 5:22)	Contented (Phil. 4:11)
Volitional	Submissive (Rom. 13:1–5)	Self-controlled (Gal. 5:23)	Disciplined (1 Tim. 4:7–8)
Relational	Accepted and forgiven (Rom. 5:8; 15:7)	Forgiving (Eph. 4:32)	Loving and unselfish (Phil. 2:1–5)

God's Story for You and *Your New Identity*, the first two studies in the VICTORY SERIES, focused on the issues that help the believer become firmly rooted in Christ (level one in above chart). If you have completed those studies, then you know the whole gospel, who you are in Christ, and who is your heavenly Father. *Your Foundation in Christ*, the third study in the VICTORY SERIES, and this study, *Renewing Your Mind*, discuss issues that are related to your growth in Christ (level two in the above chart).

As you work through the six sessions in this Bible study, you will learn how to tear down mental strongholds that keep you in bondage, allow Christ to rule in your heart, be led by the Spirit, live under grace, and overcome anger, depression and losses. Growth requires the right foundation, which is your personal identity and security in Christ. The Steps to Freedom in Christ will be mentioned during this study. This booklet can be purchased at any Christian bookstore or from Freedom in Christ Ministries. The Steps to Freedom in Christ is a repentance process that can help you resolve your personal and spiritual conflicts. The theology and application of the Steps is explained in the book *Discipleship Counseling*.

Before starting each daily reading, review the portion of Scripture listed for that day, then complete the questions at the end of each day's reading. These questions have been written to allow you to reflect on the material and apply to your life the ideas presented in the reading. At the end of each study, I have included a quote from a Church father illustrating the continuity of the Christian faith. Featured articles will appear in the text throughout the series, which are for the edification of the reader and not necessarily meant for discussion.

If you are part of a small group, be prepared to share your thoughts and insights with your group. You may also want to set up an accountability partnership with someone in your group to encourage you as you apply what you have learned in each session. For those of you who are leading a small group, there are leader tips at the end of this book that will help you guide your participants through the material.

As with any spiritual discipline, you will be tempted at times not to finish this study. There is a "sure reward" for those who make a "sure commitment." The VICTORY SERIES is far more than an intellectual exercise. The truth will not set you free if you only acknowledge it and discuss it on an intellectual level. For the truth to transform your life, you must believe it personally and allow it to sink deep into your heart. Trust the Holy Spirit to lead you into all truth and enable you to be the person God has created you to be. Decide to live what you have chosen to believe.

Dr. Neil T. Anderson

Being Transformed

Albert Einstein said, "It has become appallingly obvious that our technology has exceeded our humanity." In other words, knowledge does not equate to character, which Paul warned us about: "We know that we all possess knowledge. Knowledge puffs up, but love builds up. The man who thinks he knows something does not yet know as he ought to know" (1 Corinthians 8:1–2). When we make knowledge an end in itself, it undermines the very purpose for which it was intended. "But the goal of our instruction is love from a pure heart and a good conscience and a sincere faith" (1 Timothy 1:5 NASB). Jesus said, "By this all men will know that you are my disciples, if you love one another" (John 13:35).

The smartphone has changed the way we live. Information about almost everything is now available at our fingertips. The accumulation of knowledge is doubling every two years, but where is the personal transformation? Where has all this information led us?

Daily Readings

1. Renewing Our Minds	Romans 12:1–8
2. Tearing Down Mental Strongholds	2 Corinthians 10:1–5
3. Letting Christ Rule in Our Hearts	Psalm 119:1–16
4. Choosing the Truth	Philippians 4:4–9
5. Observing God's Word	Ezra 7:8–10

1

Renewing Our Minds

Romans 12:1–8

Key Point

Transformation begins at salvation and continues as we renew our minds.

Key Verse

And we all, who with unveiled faces contemplate the Lord's glory, are being transformed into his image with ever-increasing glory, which comes from the Lord, who is the Spirit.

2 Corinthians 3:18

M any new believers have never been part of a Christian fellowship before. In a good church the people seem friendly enough, and the people go out of their way to make new believers feel welcome. New believers are initially encouraged by the message that they are new creations in Christ. They would like to believe that, but they wonder why they still struggle with the same old issues, thoughts, and feelings. All new believers have probably wondered that—and they deserve an adequate answer.

Let's start with an illustration. Suppose you played for an abusive soccer coach. He belittled his team and ruled with fear and intimidation. In order to make the team, you had to learn how to cope, succeed, and survive under his authority. Then one day you were traded to a new team, and you got a new coach. The old coach was gone. You were no longer under his authority, and you no longer had any relationship with him.

Your new coach was nothing like your old coach. He was kind and respectful to his team, and he motivated the players out of love. But how do you think you initially related to your new coach and teammates? Probably the same way you had been trained under the old coach. Hopefully, your relationship with your new coach, your behavior on the field, and your attitude toward the game would slowly change as you got to know the new coach and learned how to be a better team player on a well-coached team.

We all started out on the wrong team. We were born physically alive but spiritually dead in our trespasses and sins (see Ephesians 2:1), and we learned how to live independently of God. We had no relationship with God and no knowledge of His ways. So we learned how to cope and tried by our own efforts to succeed in this fallen world. Having no other recourse, we "followed the ways of this world and of the ruler of the kingdom of [darkness] . . . gratifying the cravings of our flesh and following its desires and thoughts. Like the rest, we were by nature deserving of wrath" (Ephesians 2:2–3). As a result, sinful thoughts and desires were deeply ingrained in our minds.

Then one day we became new creations in Christ. We were transferred to a different team and got a new coach, but nobody pushed the "clear" button in our memory banks. All the previous training experiences, memories, and habits were still programmed into our minds, which is why Paul wrote, "Do not conform to the pattern of this world, but be transformed by the renewing of your mind" (Romans 12:2).

We all were conformed to this world. Even as believers, we will remain conformed to this world if we continue believing and living as we always have. So we must make a conscious decision to put aside the lifestyles of this "present evil age" (Galatians 1:4). We must continuously be transformed by the renewing of our minds. The English word "transformation" comes from the Greek word *metamorphosis*, which implies a total change from inside out. The key to this transformation is the mind, which is the control center of our thoughts, attitudes, and actions.

Why do believers still often struggle with many of the issues they had in their former lives before coming to Christ?

_____

_____

_____

Why are we told to lean not on our own understanding but in all ways acknowledge God?

_____

_____

_____

How do we move from information to transformation?

_____

_____

_____

How did you live under the ruler of this world as compared to living under the lordship of Christ?

_____

_____

_____

_____

15

Should you seek to be transformed in order to be accepted, or have you been accepted and need to be transformed? Explain.

_____

_____

_____

_____

"Be transformed by the renewal of your mind" tells us what form is guilty, for every soul once had the form of wickedness. . . . Our mind is renewed by the practice of wisdom and reflection on the Word of God and the spiritual understanding of the law. The more one reads the Scriptures daily and the greater one's understanding is, the more one is renewed always and every day. I doubt whether a mind which is lazy toward the Holy Scriptures and the exercise of spiritual knowledge can be renewed at all.

Origen (AD 184–253)

2

Tearing Down Mental Strongholds

2 Corinthians 10:1–5

Key Point

Before we came to Christ, we developed defense mechanisms or flesh patterns as we mentally processed the environment in which we were raised.

Key Verse

We demolish arguments and every pretension that sets itself up against the knowledge of God, and we take captive every thought to make it obedient to Christ.

2 Corinthians 10:5

The imagery Paul uses in 2 Corinthians 10:4–5 relates not to defensive armor but to battering-ram offensive weaponry. He is not using the conventional weapons of this world to tear down strongholds but the divine weapons at our disposal. These strongholds are not physical barriers that fortify a city. They are mental strongholds raised up against the knowledge of God. We can tear them down because we have the mind of Christ (see 1 Corinthians 2:16) and the Spirit of truth within us.

Research shows that we form attitudes and beliefs early in our childhood. We are not physically born with the presence of God in our lives, so we absorb these mental attitudes from our environment in two primary ways. First, we assimilate them into our minds through prevailing experiences such as the homes in which we were raised, the schools we attended, and the neighborhoods in which we played. These values and attitudes are more caught than taught. Different children respond to the same environment in different ways; therefore, every child's mental evaluation is different. Second, we develop mental strongholds through traumatic experiences like the death of a parent, divorce in the home, or various kinds of mental and physical abuse. We are not in bondage to traumatic experiences; we are in bondage to the lies we believed as a result of those experiences.

Strongholds are mental habit patterns of thought. Some call them "flesh patterns." These strongholds are memory traces burned into our minds over time or by the intensity of traumatic experiences. They are similar to what psychologists call defense mechanisms, and they always reveal themselves in a less-than-Christlike temperament. They are like deep tire tracks in a wet pasture. After the ruts have been established and dried over time, the driver doesn't have to steer anymore. The vehicle will just follow those ruts, and any attempt to steer out of them will be met with resistance. If we follow those neurological pathways for six consecutive weeks, a habit will be established. If the habit persists, a stronghold will form.

For example, an inferiority complex is a mental stronghold. Nobody is born inferior to another, but in this competitive world, it is almost impossible not to feel inferior to someone who is smarter, faster, stronger, and prettier. Negative self-perceptions can only be torn down in Christ. In the kingdom of God, everybody has equal value. God loves each of His children the same, and we are not in competition with one another.

Another example would be the unhealthy characteristics exhibited by children of an alcoholic. Suppose the oldest child chooses to stand up to his father when he comes home drunk. The middle son accommodates his father. The youngest son runs and hides. Twenty years later, those three boys are confronted by a hostile situation. Chances are the oldest son will fight, the middle son will accommodate, and the youngest son will run and hide. We learn mental strongholds like these over time as we interact with our environment, but they can be torn down in Christ.

If we have been trained wrongly, can we be retrained? If we have believed a lie, can we now believe the truth? If we have programmed our minds wrongly, can they be reprogrammed? Of course! We are transformed by the renewing of our minds.

What are the "weapons" to which Paul refers in 2 Corinthians 10:4? What do they have the power to do?

_____

_____

_____

_____

What are the two primary ways in which we form attitudes and beliefs early in our childhood?

_____

_____

_____

_____

How can we overcome flesh patterns/defense mechanisms?

_____

_____

_____

_____

How can you tell when your response to others is a flesh pattern?

_____

_____

_____

Now that you are a new creation in Christ, why don't you need old defense mechanisms such as lying, blaming, or denying?

_____

_____

_____

Here, also, one who examines each word minutely can gain a very accurate knowledge of the meaning of the Holy Scripture, so that there is no excuse for any of us being led astray into the snare of sin by an erroneous belief that some sins are punished while others may be committed with impunity. For, what says the apostle? "Destroying counsels and every height that exalts itself against the knowledge of God"; so that every sin, because it is an expression of contempt for the divine law, is called a "height that exalts itself against the knowledge of God."

Basil the Great (AD 330–379)

3

Letting Christ Rule
in Our Hearts

Psalm 119:1–16

Key Point

Christ rules in our hearts when we let the Word of Christ richly dwell within us.

Key Verse

Let the peace of Christ rule in your hearts, since as members of one body you were called to peace. And be thankful.

Colossians 3:15

Psalm 119 is a devotional on the Word of God. It has 22 divisions, each beginning with a different letter in the Hebrew alphabet. The psalmist asks, "How can a young person stay on the path of purity? By living according to your word. . . . I have hidden your word in my heart that I might not sin against you" (verses 9, 11). Paul expands on this instruction in Colossians 3:15: "Let the peace of Christ rule in your hearts." "Rule" means "to act as a judge or arbiter." How do we let the peace of

Christ arbitrate in our hearts? By letting the Word of Christ dwell within us (see Colossians 3:16).

Let's say you have stored a lot of filth in your mind and then one day you decide to clean up your mind. The battle gets worse the moment you make that decision. The battle isn't very intense as long as you are just giving in to tempting thoughts. The battle begins the moment you decide to resist tempting thoughts. So how do you win the battle for your mind?

Imagine your mind is a pot filled with coffee. Because you chose to mix coffee grounds with the water, the liquid is dark, dirty, and opaque. There is no way you can filter out the coffee from the water. Now suppose there is a bowl of crystal-clear ice next to the pot. Each day, you take one ice cube and put it in the pot. At first you do not notice any difference, but as you add one cube per day, the liquid in the pot begins to clear up. If you keep adding ice day after day, there will come a time when you won't be able to taste, smell, or see the coffee in the pot. Although the coffee is still there, the ice has diluted it. This method will only work if you don't also keep adding a scoop of coffee every day.

If we wish to rid our minds of filth, we must read and study the Word of God each day. Our minds are like computers—if we put garbage in, we will get garbage out. The process of renewing our mind often begins with one step forward and one step backward. We spend time in God's Word during our devotions, but then go back into the world for work and leisure, where we are mentally assaulted again. Learning to take every thought captive in obedience to Christ takes time and commitment, but it can be done. The next day we take two steps forward and one back, then three steps forward and one back. If we stay committed to the process, it will soon become 20, 30, and 40 steps forward and one back.

The Spirit of God will lead us into all truth if we choose that path, and He will convict us if we choose the wrong path. Make a commitment to be like the psalmist, who wrote, "I rejoice in following your statutes as one rejoices in great riches. I meditate on your precepts and consider your ways. I delight in your decrees; I will not neglect your word" (Psalm 119:14–16).

Why will the battle for our minds get worse the moment we make a decision to rid ourselves of thoughts not from God?

How can we begin to rid our minds of filth since there is no "delete" button?

Why is it important not to get discouraged as we begin the process of renewing our minds?

What is your worst mental obsession? How did it start?

What practical steps can you take so that the peace of Christ can rule in your heart?

_____

_____

_____

Seek nothing with exterior gold and bodily adornment; but consider the garment as one worthy to adorn him who is according to the image of his Creator, as the apostle says, "Stripping off the old man, and putting on the new, one that is being renewed unto perfect knowledge 'according to the image of his Creator.'" And he who had put on "the heart of mercy, kindness, humility, patience and meekness" is clothed within and has adorned the inner man.

Basil the Great (AD 330–379)

4

Choosing the Truth
Philippians 4:4–9

Key Point

We are not called to dispel the darkness; we are called to turn on the light.

Key Verse

Whatever you have learned or received or heard from me, or seen in me—put it into practice. And the God of peace will be with you.

Philippians 4:9

Being transformed by the renewing of our minds requires a proper orientation toward God. Circumstances may not always allow us to be happy, but we can always rejoice in the Lord. Joy is a fruit of the Spirit, and this inner joy can be experienced in every circumstance, because "the Lord is near" (Philippians 4:5).

Paul admonishes us to turn to God when we are feeling anxious, or double-minded. He then uses four words to describe how we do that. "Prayer" is a general term describing our approach to God. "Petition" is a request for a specific need. "Thanksgiving" is an attitude of the heart that should accompany prayer. "Requests" is plural and identifies what is needed. It is like saying, *Dear heavenly Father, I am anxious and in need right now. Thank You for your love, and I humbly request the following . . .* Then "the peace of God, which transcends all understanding, will guard [our] hearts and [our] minds in Christ Jesus" (verse 7).

Being created in the image of God, we have the capacity to choose. We can choose to believe or not believe, and we can choose what we want to think about. It is not enough to turn to God; we have to assume responsibility for our own thoughts. God will assist us through His grace, but He will not do our thinking for us. Paul wrote, "Whatever is true, whatever is noble, whatever is right, whatever is pure, whatever is lovely, whatever is admirable—if anything is excellent or praiseworthy—think about such things" (Philippians 4:8).

Don't try to rebuke every negative thought. That would be like trying to keep 12 corks submerged while treading water in the ocean. We should ignore the corks and swim to shore! We are not called to dispel the darkness. We are called to turn on the light. We win the battle for our minds by choosing the truth. Trying not to think negative thoughts is futile, because it just reinforces the negative thought.

Everything we do is a product of our thoughts. In other words, we don't do anything without first thinking it, which is why turning to God and thinking positive thoughts is not quite enough either. Paul continues, "Whatever you have learned or received or heard from me, or seen in me— put it into practice. And the God of peace will be with you" (verse 9). In other words, live the truth, do the noble deed, do the right thing, live a pure life, and practice loving others as a noble citizen in God's kingdom.

If we want to be transformed by the renewing of our minds, we have to reprogram our minds. However, like a computer, we better check for viruses. Computer viruses are not accidental—they have been intentionally and maliciously introduced to cripple the computer (brain) and disrupt the program (mind). "The Spirit clearly says that in later times some will abandon the faith and follow deceiving spirits and things taught by demons" (1 Timothy 4:1). That is presently happening today all over the world, which is why we need to submit to God *and* resist the devil (see

James 4:7). The Steps to Freedom in Christ have been designed to help you do that by resolving personal and spiritual conflicts through genuine repentance and faith in God.

Why can believers always rejoice in the Lord?

_____

_____

_____

What should we do when we are struggling with anxious thoughts?

_____

_____

_____

Why is it futile to try to rebuke every negative thought?

_____

_____

_____

How can you make turning to God a habit whenever you have anxious thoughts?

_____

_____

_____

Why is it so important to learn to take every thought captive in obedience to Christ?

_____

_____

_____

The devil, however, as he is the apostate angel, can only go to this length, as he did at the beginning, to deceive and lead astray the mind of man into disobeying the commandments of God, and gradually to darken the hearts.

Irenaeus (AD 130–202)

5

Observing God's Word
Ezra 7:8–10

Key Point

If we want God to transform us and renew our minds, we have to study His Word.

Key Verse

Do your best to present yourself to God as one approved, a worker who does not need to be ashamed and who correctly handles the word of truth.

2 Timothy 2:15

If we are going to be transformed by the renewing of our minds, we have to know and allow God's Word to enter our hearts. We must replace old ways of living in this world with new ways of living in the kingdom of God and the lies of this world with the truth of God's Word. It is not enough to think about Scripture; we have to think scripturally. Wisdom is seeing life from God's perspective, and we can only learn that from His Word.

29

Ezra devoted himself to studying God's Word, but he also took the next step—the most important part of learning. Ezra *observed* the law of the Lord (see Ezra 7:10). People retain only about 10 percent of what they hear and 20 percent of what they see, but they retain 90 percent of what they do. James wrote, "Do not merely listen to the word, and so deceive yourselves. Do what it says. Anyone who listens to the word but does not do what it says is like someone who looks at his face in a mirror and, after looking at himself, goes away and immediately forgets what he looks like. But whoever looks intently into the perfect law that gives freedom, and continues in it—not forgetting what they have heard, but doing it—they will be blessed in what they do" (James 1:22–25).

Nowhere is this more emphasized than in the Jewish confession of faith known as the *Shema. Shema* is the Hebrew word for "hear," and it means "to hear as though to obey." It is recorded in Deuteronomy and recited daily by pious Jews: "Hear, O Israel: The Lord our God, the Lord is one. Love the Lord your God with all your heart and with all your soul and with all your strength. These commandments that I give you today are to be on your hearts. Impress them on your children. Talk about them when you sit at home and when you walk along the road, when you lie down and when you get up. Tie them as symbols on your hands and bind them on your foreheads. Write them on the doorframes of your houses and on your gates" (6:4–9).

Paul reveals another critical reason why the knowledge of God's Word is not transforming our lives: "I gave you milk to drink, not solid food; for you were not yet able to receive it. Indeed, even now you are not yet able, for you are still fleshly. For since there is jealousy and strife among you, are you not fleshly, and are you not walking like mere men?" (1 Corinthians 3:2–3 NASB). If there is no way for Christians to resolve the jealousy and strife, they will not be able to fully receive God's Word so as to transform their lives.

David discovered this only after Nathan confronted him about his sin, and he repented. David would then write, "Yet you desired faithfulness even in the womb; you taught me wisdom in that secret place. . . . Blessed is the one whose transgressions are forgiven, whose sins are covered. Blessed is the one whose sin the LORD does not count against them and in whose spirit is no deceit" (Psalm 51:6; 32:1–2). Truth incarnated sets you free!

Why must we go beyond intellectual knowledge if we desire to be transformed?

Why does the Bible refer most often to meditating on the Law or God's Word?

How can we retain the image we see in the mirror that the Bible reflects back to those who read it?

In what way is God's Word like milk to you because of unresolved conflicts?

Have you ever heard a good message or read a chapter in the Bible and it had no lasting impact on you? Why do you think that was the case?

_____

_____

_____

A sound mind . . . that is devoted to piety and love of truth will eagerly meditate upon those things that God has placed within the power of mankind and has subjected to our knowledge. . . . Such a mind will advance in the knowledge of those things . . . by means of daily study. I am referring to those things that fall under our observation and are clearly and unambiguously set forth in the sacred Scriptures in clear terms.

Irenaeus (AD 130–202)

The Steps to Freedom in Christ

Personal and spiritual conflicts are resolved through genuine repentance and faith in God. This can't happen apart from God because He is the One who grants repentance (see 2 Timothy 2:25). Only Jesus can set captives free and bind up the wounds of the brokenhearted. The Steps to Freedom in Christ ("the Steps") were developed to facilitate this ministry of reconciliation. It is an encounter with God that an individual can process on his or her own. However, it is more effective if a trained encourager leads an inquirer through the Steps. The biblical basis and process are taught in *Discipleship Counseling.*

A Christian therapist did three pilot studies in 1996. All three of these studies were performed on participants who attended a *Living Free in Christ* conference and were led through the Steps. That conference is now the basic *Freedom in Christ Discipleship Course* that is available in a number of languages and used all over the world. The first four books of the Vic-TORY SERIES cover the same material that was taught in the conference.

The first study involved 30 participants who took a 10-item question-naire before completing the Steps. The questionnaire was re-administered three months after their participation. The questionnaire assessed for levels of depression, anxiety, inner conflict, tormenting thoughts, and addictive behaviors. The second study involved 55 participants who took a 12-item questionnaire before completing the Steps and then again 3 months later. The third pilot study involved 21 participants who also took a 12-item questionnaire before receiving the Steps and then again 3 months afterward. The following table illustrates the average percentage of improvement for each category.

	Depression	Anxiety	Inner Conflict	Tormenting Thoughts	Addictive Behavior
Pilot Study 1	64%	58%	63%	82%	52%
Pilot Study 2	47%	44%	51%	58%	43%
Pilot Study 3	52%	47%	48%	57%	39%

In each case, the encourager was a well-trained layperson who led par-ticipants through the Steps in one extended session. No further counseling or discipling took place. Research was also conducted at two additional conferences by a medical doctor and two doctor of psychology students using psychologically normed tests. A personal session conducted by a lay encourager was offered to those who asked for help. They were given a pre-test before a Step session and a post-test three months later, with the following results given in percentage of improvement:

	Oklahoma City, OK	Tyler, TX
Depression	44%	52%
Anxiety	45%	44%
Fear	48%	49%
Anger	36%	55%
Tormenting Thoughts	51%	27%
Negative Habits	48%	43%
Sense of Self-Worth	52%	40%

Living Under Grace

I felt the ingratitude, the danger, the sin of not living nearer to God. I prayed, agonized, strove, and made resolutions, read the word more diligently, sought more time for meditation—but all without avail. Every day, almost every hour, the consciousness of sin oppressed me. I knew that if I could abide in Christ all would be well, but I could not . . . Each day brought its register of sin, failure and lack of power. To will was indeed present within me, but how to perform I found not . . . I hated myself, my sin, yet I gained no strength against it.

When my agony of soul was at its height, a sentence in a letter from dear McCarthy was used to remove the scales from my eyes, and the Spirit of God revealed to me the truth of our oneness with Jesus as I had never known it before. "But how to get faith strengthened? Not by striving after faith, but by resting on the Faithful One." As I read, I saw it all! "If we believe not, He abideth faithful." I looked to Jesus and saw (and when I saw, oh, how the joy flowed) that He had said, "I will never leave thee." I thought, I have striven in vain to rest in Him, I'll strive no more. . . . But I am dead, buried with Christ—aye, and risen too![1]

—Hudson Taylor

Daily Readings

1. Dead to Sin	Romans 6:1–14
2. The Christian's Relationship to the Law	Mark 2:23–28
3. Walking With God	Matthew 11:28–30
4. Led by the Spirit	Exodus 13:17–22
5. Enduring Hardship	Hebrews 12:1–13

1

Dead to Sin

Romans 6:1–14

Key Point

We are no longer slaves to sin, because we are alive in Christ and dead to sin.

Key Verse

If we have been united with [Christ] in a death like his, we will certainly also be united with him in a resurrection like his.

Romans 6:5

Biblical commands should be obeyed. Biblical promises should be claimed. However, the only appropriate response to biblical fact or truth is to believe it! The first 10 verses in Romans 6 declare the truth about our spiritual union with Christ. We choose to believe that Christ has triumphed over sin and death, and so have we, because we are alive "in Christ."

"We are those who have died to sin; how can we live in it any longer?" (Romans 6:2). How can we as believers "die to sin"? We can't, because we already have. "Or don't you know that all of us who were baptized into Christ Jesus were baptized into his death?" (verse 3). We have also been buried and raised with Christ (see verses 4–5). We cannot be united with Christ in His death and not be united with Him in His resurrected life. Jesus didn't just die for our sins; He also came to give us life: "Now if we died with Christ, we believe that we will also live with him" (verse 8).

Although Scripture tells us that we died with Christ, the defeated Christian tries to put the old self to death but can't do it. Why? Because he or she is already dead! "For we know that our old self was crucified with him" (verse 6). It is false reasoning to ask what experience we must have for this to be true. The only experience that had to happen took place 2,000 years ago, and the only way we can enter into the experience is by faith. We cannot do for ourselves what Christ has already done for us. We don't make anything true by our experience. We believe that what God has done and said on our behalf is true. When we choose to believe God and live accordingly by faith, it works out in our experience.

We don't do the things we do with the hope that God may someday love us. God loves us, and that is why we do the good things we do. We don't labor in the vineyard with the hope that God may someday accept us. God has accepted us, and that is why we labor in the vineyard. What we do does not determine who we are. God has determined who we are, and being new creations in Christ should determine what we do. When we choose to sin, it does not make us sinners any more than sneezing makes us sneezers.

Christ defeated death when He was resurrected, and He defeated sin when He died once for all our sins (see Romans 6:8–10). "In the same way, count yourselves dead to sin but alive to God in Christ Jesus" (verse 11). Counting ourselves dead to sin does not make us dead to sin. We are dead to sin because of our new life in Christ; therefore, we continue to believe it, and it will work out in our experience. Sin is still powerful and appealing, but our relationship with sin has changed. When we are tempted to sin, we should respond by faith and say, "I am alive in Christ, and sin is no longer my master."

What does Paul mean in Romans 6:2 when he states that believers have "died to sin"? How have they triumphed over sin and death?

_____

_____

_____

_____

What happens when we try to do for ourselves what Christ has already done for us?

_____

_____

_____

_____

What is our motivation for believing God and living accordingly by faith?

_____

_____

_____

Have you ever fallen into the trap of believing that what you do determines who you are? Explain.

_____

_____

_____

_____

How can you stand up to Satan's temptations?

_____

_____

_____

Whoever thinks or considers that he is dead will not sin. For example, if lust for a woman gets hold of me or greed for silver, gold or riches stirs me and I say in my heart that I have died with Christ . . . the lust is immediately quenched and sin disappears. The addition of "alive to God in Christ Jesus" does not seem to me to be superfluous. It is as if Paul were saying that we are alive to God in wisdom, peace, righteousness and sanctification, all of which Christ is. Living to God in these is the same as living to God in Christ Jesus. For as nobody lives to God without righteousness, peace, sanctification and the other virtues, so it is certain that no one can live to God except in Christ Jesus.

Origen (AD 184–253)

2

The Christian's Relationship to the Law

Mark 2:23–28

Key Point

The letter of the law kills, but the Spirit gives life.

Key Verse

We have been released from the law so that we serve in the new way of the Spirit, and not in the old way of the written code.

Romans 7:6

The Pharisees were strict in keeping the law, but they added many rules and regulations that were intended to keep believers from breaking the law. Their tactic was similar to building a fence around the law, but in practice the fence itself soon became a law. We do the same thing today. For instance, in 2 Corinthians 6:14 we are told not to be unequally yoked. So, to keep our Christian children from marrying a nonbeliever, we establish additional rules like, "You can't date nonbelievers or associate with them."

That may be wise in some cases, but it is not a law. Jesus ignored man-made rules, but He never violated the law. In fact, Jesus said, "Do not think that I have come to abolish the Law or the Prophets; I have not come to abolish them but to fulfill them" (Matthew 5:17). How, then, do we as believers relate to the law?

The term "law" in Scripture is often associated with specific commands, especially the Old Testament Mosaic Law. But the concept of law is much broader. The Hebrew word *torah*, which is the basic word for "law" in the Old Testament, is related to the Hebrew word *hora*, meaning "to teach or instruct." The fundamental meaning is not "command" but "instruct." The word eventually came to be used for the entire Word of God. The Jews use the word "Torah" to refer to the first five books of the Old Testament. Christians have used the term "law" to describe sections of Scripture and Scripture as a whole, including commandments as well as promises. The latter is what Jesus meant when He said that He came to fulfill the Law. He kept all the commandments and fulfilled all the promises.

The law of God is an expression of His will. Just as there are physical laws that govern nature, so there are His moral and spiritual laws, which are the expression of His moral nature, that govern the personal and moral spheres of God's creation. For this reason, in the Old Testament both believers and unbelievers were subject to the overarching principle that following God's laws led to blessings, while disobeying them led to misery and destruction.

New Testament believers "in Christ" are not related to the law in the same way. Nonbelievers stand before the law in themselves—that is, as sinners and, consequently, lawbreakers. They live under the condemnation of the law. But believers "in Christ" have the same relationship to the law as Christ. God's righteous principles for life are all fulfilled in Christ. We are free from the legal bondage of the law. "Therefore, there is now no condemnation for those who are in Christ Jesus" (Romans 8:1).

The law became our tutor to lead us to Christ so we could be justified by faith (see Galatians 3:24–25). Now that we are alive in Christ, the law is no longer our tutor. What we could not fulfill in the flesh, Christ fulfilled for us. Now that we are "in Christ," we can actually live righteous lives that are consistent with the moral laws of God. However, the means by which we attempt to live righteously have changed. We now relate to God by faith, and live by the power of the Holy Spirit who is our Tutor.

Why did the Pharisees add rules and regulations to the law? How do we do the same thing today?

_____

_____

_____

What does the concept of "the law" in Scripture encompass?

_____

_____

_____

How were Old Testament believers related to the law? How are New Testament believers related to the law?

_____

_____

_____

How have the commandments of the law become promises for you—for instance, "Thou shall not steal or kill" to "I will not steal or kill"?

_____

_____

_____

How has living by the letter of the law kept you from living a liberated life?

_____

_____

_____

Therefore, you that fear the Lord, praise Him, and that you may worship Him, not as slaves but as free men, learn to love Him whom you fear, and you will be able to praise what you love. The men of the Old Testament, fearing God, because of the letter [of the law], which terrifies and kills and not yet possessing "the Spirit that quickens," ran to the temple with sacrifices and offered up bloody victims. They were ignorant of what was foreshadowed by them, although they were a figure of the Blood to come, by which we have been redeemed.

Augustine of Hippo (AD 354–430)

3

Walking With God

Matthew 11:28–30

Key Point

We have been invited to walk with the gentle Jesus.

Key Verse

Walk with the wise and become wise, for a companion of fools suffers harm.

Proverbs 13:20

How much can we accomplish in the kingdom of God when we operate by ourselves? Nothing! How much can we accomplish in this present Church Age if we do nothing and expect God to do everything? Nothing! God has committed Himself to work through the Church. We have the privilege to water and plant in God's kingdom, "but God [makes] it grow" (1 Corinthians 3:6). Nothing grows without God, but nothing grows if we don't water and plant. The fact that nobody hears unless a preacher is sent (see Romans 10:14–15) illustrates the same principle. God could have chosen to bypass the Church, but He has chosen to work through us. It is His intention that we walk together, and Jesus has provided the perfect example of how that works.

Jesus was a carpenter during His youth, and His handiwork later became useful metaphors for His ministry. Carpenters didn't frame houses in those days; they fashioned doors and yokes out of wood. A yoke is a heavy wooden beam that fits over the shoulders of two oxen. The yoke can only work if two oxen are in it and are pulling together. For the purpose of training, a young ox is yoked to an older ox that has "learned obedience from what he suffered" (Hebrews 5:8).

The young ox will be tempted to stray off to the left or to the right, but the old ox stays on the right path. The young ox may think the pace is too slow and try running ahead, but all he gets is a sore neck. Slowly, the young ox begins to realize the old ox knows how to walk. The pace is right and the course is true, so he decides to learn from him. "Though youths grow weary and tired, and vigorous young men stumble badly, yet those who wait for the LORD will gain new strength; they will mount up with wings like eagles, they will run and not get tired, they will walk and not become weary" (Isaiah 40:30–31 NASB).

Being yoked with Jesus does not mean we sit around thinking pious thoughts expecting God to do it all. Nor does it mean running around in endless activities trying to do it all by ourselves. It is a walk with the only One who knows the way, who is the truth, and has the life to make it possible. In Him we find rest for our souls, for His yoke is easy and His burden is light (see Matthew 11:29–30).

What would we learn from Jesus if we walked with Him? We would learn to take one day at a time and trust God for tomorrow (see Matthew 6:25–34). We would learn the priority of relationships. We would learn to love people and use things—instead of loving things and using people. We would learn what it means to be compassionate. Jesus said, "Go and learn with this means: 'I desire mercy, not sacrifice'" (Matthew 9:13).

This passage in Matthew 11:28–30 is the only place in the Bible where Jesus describes Himself, and He says, "I am gentle and humble in heart" (verse 29). With all the harshness and vulgarity surrounding us in this fallen world, we have been invited to walk with the gentle Jesus. Imagine that!

Why shouldn't we ask or expect God to do all the work in the kingdom?

_____

_____

_____

Why do we try to build God's kingdom for Him instead of waiting on the Lord?

_____

_____

_____

_____

What is the practical significance of being yoked to Jesus? How does that work?

_____

_____

_____

_____

What is your tendency as a young Christian when yoked together with God? To run on ahead? To drop out? To stray off to the left or right?

_____

_____

_____

_____

Is being yoked together with God a liberating or binding concept to you? Why?

_____

_____

_____

Draw near to Me, so that you may become sharers of the divine nature and partakers of the Holy Spirit. Jesus called everyone, not only the people of Israel. As the Maker and Lord of all, He spoke to the weary Jews who did not have the strength to bear the yoke of the law. He spoke to idolators heavy laden and oppressed by the devil and weighed down by the multitude of their sins. To Jews He said, "Obtain the profit of my coming to you. Bow down to the truth. Acknowledge your Advocate and Lord. I set you free from bondage under the law, bondage in which you endured a great deal of toil and hardship, unable to accomplish it easily and accumulating for yourselves a very great burden of sin."

Cyril of Alexandria (AD 376–444)

4

Led by the Spirit

Exodus 13:17–22

Key Point

The sheep of God's pasture know the voice of the Good Shepherd and follow Him.

Key Verse

Those who are led by the Spirit of God are the children of God.

Romans 8:14

Even in the wilderness, God led His people and provided for their needs. He guided them with a cloud by day and a pillar of fire by night (see Exodus 13:20–22), and He never deserted them. His guidance was unfailing, constant and loving. "He brought his people out like a flock; he led them like sheep through the wilderness" (Psalm 78:52). "We are his people, the sheep of his pasture" (100:3), and Jesus is "the good shepherd" (John 10:14). "He calls his own sheep by name and leads them out" (verse 3).

In Scripture, God's children are often referred to as sheep. For the most part this is a comforting notion, but it also conveys our helplessness. Sheep are not carnivorous like wolves. They sacrificially give their wool while they are living and their meat when they die. There is a lot of good to be said for sheep, but they are not the smartest animals on the farm. When left alone in lush green pastures, sheep will eat themselves to death. Perhaps this is why David tells us, "The LORD is my shepherd, I lack nothing. He *makes me lie down* in green pastures" (Psalm 23:1–2, emphasis added).

In our Western world, we keep our sheep moving in green pastures by chasing them from the rear. But that is not the way shepherds led their sheep in Israel. Even to this day, the shepherd will let the sheep graze until they are full or in need of greener pastures. The shepherd will then stand up, say something, and then walk away. The sheep will look up and follow the shepherd. That is why Jesus says, "My sheep listen to my voice; I know them, and they follow me" (John 10:27). Paul writes, "Those who are led by the Spirit of God are the children of God" (Romans 8:14).

Being led by the Spirit implies that we are not being pushed. So if someone asks you to make a hasty decision without prayerful reflection, the answer should be no. God doesn't lead that way. God's guidance may come suddenly but never to the spiritually unprepared. Pentecost was sudden, but it was preceded by many days of prayer (see Acts 1:14).

Being led by the Spirit also means that we are not being lured away in some clandestine manner. God does everything in the light, but Satan is the prince of darkness. In the same epistle in which Paul tells us we are seated with Christ in the heavenlies (the spiritual realm), we are also told that we will have to stand firm "against the spiritual forces of evil in the heavenly realms" (Ephesians 6:12).

To guard against deception we must put on the armor of God, and we start with the belt of truth. The only way to recognize the counterfeit is to know the truth. John wrote, "We know that we are children of God, and that the whole world is under the control of the evil one. We know also that the Son of God has come and has given us understanding, so that we may know him who is true" (1 John 5:19–20). Jesus said, "I am the good shepherd; I know my sheep and my sheep know me . . . and I lay down my life for the sheep" (John 10:14–15).

What lessons can we learn from the metaphor that we are the sheep of His pasture?

How did shepherds in Jesus' day lead their sheep? What should we learn from that?

Why must we put on the armor of God?

How can you detect counterfeit guidance?

How can you get to know the voice of God?

_____

_____

_____

The whole essence of the Gospel is to think according to the Spirit, to live according to the Spirit, to believe according to the Spirit, to have nothing of the flesh in one's mind and acts and life. That means also to have no hope in the flesh. "Walk then," he says, "in the Spirit"—that is, "Be alive. If you do so you will not consummate the desires of the flesh. You will admit into consciousness no sin, which is born of the flesh."

Gaius Marius Victorinus (c. fourth century AD)

5

Enduring Hardship
Hebrews 12:1–13

Key Point

To fulfill our purpose in life, we must persevere in Christ even in the face of hardship.

Key Verse

You therefore must endure hardship as a good soldier of Jesus Christ.

2 Timothy 2:3 NKJV

Bringing light into a dark world invites three predictable responses in people. First, some will run from the light because their deeds are evil. Jesus said, "Everyone who does evil hates the light, and will not come into the light for fear that their deeds will be exposed" (John 3:20). Those who live in sin feel convicted around Christians, so they stay away from churches that preach the truth. Second, some will embrace the light as a liberating friend and gladly come to Jesus. Third, some will try to discredit the light source. This is what men tried to do to Jesus, and those who let their light shine today will suffer from similar insults and persecution.

The writer of Hebrews states, "Remember those earlier days after you had received the light, when you endured in a great conflict full of suffering. Sometimes you were publicly exposed to insult and persecution; at other times you stood side by side with those who were so treated" (10:32–33). With such opposition, how do we "run with perseverance the race marked out for us" (12:1)?

First, we consider the example of Jesus, who is the author and perfecter of our faith. Nobody suffered like Jesus did for the sake of righteousness. He is our model and inspiration for endurance. "Consider him who endured such opposition from sinners, so that you will not grow weary and lose heart" (verse 3). Second, we consider the example of the heroes of faith mentioned in Hebrews 11—the great cloud of witnesses cheering us on to victory. If they could endure ill treatment without having the life of Christ in them, imagine what we can endure. We should always keep in mind that the will of God will never lead us where the grace of God cannot sustain us.

Third, we are to "endure hardship as discipline" (Hebrews 12:7). Being disciplined by God proves we are His children, "because the Lord disciplines the one he loves" (verse 6). If we as imperfect parents are aware of the need to discipline our children, how much more aware is God of *our* need for discipline? We can endure hardship as discipline if we know there is a purpose behind it. "No discipline seems pleasant at the time, but painful. Later on, however, it produces a harvest of righteousness and peace for those who have been trained by it" (verse 11).

Those who prosper in life know that endurance is the key to success. It is said that success is 10 percent inspiration and 90 percent perspiration. Those who earn graduate degrees are usually no more intelligent than those who quit before they finish their program; they graduated because they endured the process. No pain, no gain—this is true not just of the athlete but also for those who have overcome the odds to be all that Christ created them to be.

You will never fulfill your purpose in life if you choose the path of least resistance or quit before you finish the race. Too many Christians encounter a little opposition and drop out, saying, "It must not be God's will." On the contrary, it is God's will that you persevere. "You need to persevere so that when you have done the will of God, you will receive what he has promised" (Hebrews 10:36).

What three responses can we expect from others when confronted with the light of Christ?

_____

_____

_____

According to the writer of Hebrews, what opposition will we face in life?

_____

_____

_____

What are three ways we can persevere when faced with difficulties?

_____

_____

_____

_____

In what ways have you been tempted to "drop out" when things get too hard and not follow the course you know God has set for you?

_____

_____

_____

_____

How have you benefited from persevering through challenges?

"You must therefore endure rough times as a good soldier of Jesus Christ." . . . Observe the kings on earth, how great an honor it is esteemed to serve under them. If therefore the soldier of the king ought to endure hardness, not to endure hardness is not the part of a soldier.

John Chrysostom (AD 347–407)

Renouncing

When making a public profession of faith, members of the Early Church would stand, face the west, and say, "I renounce you, Satan, and all your works, and all your ways." This declaration is still practiced by many expressions of Christianity throughout the world. They began the repentance process by renouncing every counterfeit religious experience they had, every false vow or pledge they made, and every false teacher or doctrine in which they believed. They would then face the east and make a public declaration to follow Christ and believe the truth.

It was understood in the Old Testament that "whoever conceals their sins does not prosper, but the one who confesses and renounces them finds mercy" (Proverbs 28:13). Paul also encouraged the Church to renounce secret and shameful ways and choose the truth (see 2 Corinthians 4:1–2). Renunciation involves giving up a claim or right. When we renounce something, we are making a definite decision to let go of any past unrighteous commitments, pledges, vows, pacts, and beliefs that are not Christian.

We have not truly repented (changed our mind) if we make a decision for Christ and continue to hold on to the past and believe what we have always believed. That would make salvation an experience of addition rather than transformation. To decisively let go of the past is the first step in repentance.

New believers can easily lose heart if they simply add a little Christianity to their existing world experience. The finished work of Christ atoned for our sins and provided new life in Christ. However, the moment we were born again, we had not fully repented, nor were our minds instantly renewed. We needed the Holy Spirit within us to lead us to the truth that would set us free. Only then could we fully repent and be transformed by the renewing of our minds. As new believers, we can repent because it is God who grants repentance that leads to a knowledge of the truth. Only then can we come to our senses and escape the trap of the devil (see 2 Timothy 2:25–26). Failure to do so will leave many Christians defeated and bound to their pasts.

Overcoming Anger

"Disappointment—His appointment," change one letter, then I see,
   That the thwarting of my purpose is God's better choice for me.
His appointment must be blessing, though it may come in disguise,
   For the end from the beginning open to His wisdom lies.
"Dissappointment—His appointment," Whose? The Lord, who loves me best,
   Undertstands and knows me fully, who my faith and love would test;
For, like a loving earthly parent, He rejoices when He knows
   That His child accepts, unquestioned, all that from His wisdom flows.
"Disappointment—His appointment," no good thing will He withhold,
   From denials oft we gather treasures of His love untold.
Well He knows each broken purpose leads to fuller, deeper trust,
   And the end of all His dealings proves our God is wise and just.
"Disappointment—His appointment," Lord, I take it, then, as such.
   Like the Rod in hands of potter, yielding wholly to Thy touch.
All my life's plan is Thy molding; not one single choice be mine;
   Let me answer, unrepining—"Father, not my will, but Thine."

                                             —Edith Lillian Young

Daily Readings

1. Emotional Honesty	1 Samuel 18:1–16
2. A Humble Walk With God	Micah 6:6–8
3. Goals and Desires	Luke 12:13–21
4. A True Sense of Worth	2 Peter 1:3–11
5. Righteous Indignation	Mark 11:12–25

1

Emotional Honesty
1 Samuel 18:1–16

Key Point

We need to be real about our emotional condition if we want to be right with God.

Key Verses

"In your anger do not sin": Do not let the sun go down while you are still angry, and do not give the devil a foothold.

Ephesians 4:26–27

Think of your emotions as being to your soul what your ability to feel is to your body. Now suppose somebody had the power to take away the sensation of physical pain and offered it to you as a gift. Would you receive it? If you lost the ability to feel pain, your body would become hopelessly scarred in a short time. Your soul would also be scarred if you never felt anger, anxiety, or depression.

These God-given emotions are like an indicator light on the dash of a car. Covering the light with a piece of tape is like suppressing our emotions, which is dishonest and unhealthy. Stuffing our emotions will cause psychosomatic illnesses. Smashing the light is indiscriminate expression, and venting our rage is unhealthy for the people around us. So, how should we deal with our emotions? What we should do is look under the hood of the car. That is acknowledgment. Our emotional health is dependent on our emotional honesty. We can't be right with God and not be real. If necessary, God may have to make us real in order to be right with Him.

When it comes to learning about how to deal with our anger, we can learn some valuable lessons from the story of Saul and David. Saul was jealous of David because David was getting more applause than he was. Like many insecure people, he grew angry because David was upstaging his social status. Saul certainly didn't look under the hood, nor did he suppress his anger. He vented his anger on David. A little self-inventory may have prevented all of that.

David was the best friend of Saul's son. David had saved Israel from the Philistine giant, and he had successfully done whatever Saul sent him to do (see 1 Samuel 18:5). Saul should have thanked God for David. David was secure because the Lord was with him (see verse 12). People who are secure in Christ are less prone to anger because their identity and sense of worth are found in Christ, not in the success or failure of others or in the positive or negative circumstances of life.

Before Saul ever became angry with David, he was bitter as a result of his confrontation with Samuel (see 1 Samuel 15). Because of Saul's rebellion and disobedience, the Lord had rejected Saul as king of Israel and told Samuel to anoint David as king. There is no evidence that Saul ever repented of his sin or forgave David for upstaging him. At the heart of an angry person is a bitter spirit, and such unresolved anger gives the devil an opportunity. After venting his anger toward David, "The next day an evil spirit from God came forcefully on Saul" (1 Samuel 18:10). The same could happen to us if we do not forgive from our heart.

Paul advises us, "'In your anger do not sin': Do not let the sun go down while you are still angry, and do not give the devil a foothold" (Ephesians 4:26–27). Our spiritual and mental health depends on how well we learn to handle our emotions. It is not a sin to be angry, but in our anger we must not sin. If we wish not to sin, then we should be angry the way Christ was: We should be angry at sin.

How do we hurt ourselves when we suppress our emotions? How does that affect our communication with others, since most communication is nonverbal?

How can we hurt others if we indiscriminately express our feelings?

What was the root of Saul's anger?

How did your parents express themselves emotionally? How has that affected you?

How does your ability to be emotionally honest reflect your security in Christ?

_____

_____

_____

The devil can do nothing to us unless we ourselves willingly allow him to do so. This is true in all our acts. Thus we are masters of our own will; otherwise we would deserve no good return for our good acts, and no punishment for our bad acts. The devil's opporunity arises from our own vice.

Gaius Marius Victorinus (c. fourth century AD)

2

A Humble Walk With God

Micah 6:6–8

Key Point

No God-given goal for your life can be blocked, uncertain, or impossible.

Key Verse

Make it your ambition to lead a quiet life: You should mind your own business and work with your hands, just as we told you.

1 Thessalonians 4:11

The process of walking by faith can be illustrated by the game of golf. Suppose a five-year-old child hits the ball 75 yards but is 15 degrees off the center of the fairway. Because of the short distance, the ball will probably land in the fairway. When the child is 12 years old, he hits the ball 200 yards but again is 15 degrees off. Now the ball is probably in the rough. When the child becomes an adult and hits the ball 300 yards, a 15-degree error could land the ball out of bounds.

If what we believe is 15 degrees off from the Word of God, there may not be many negative consequences when we are young. However, there will be consequences if we continue on that course through midlife. We end up playing out of the rough or being penalized for being out of bounds. The midlife crisis is a plan led astray. There are near and far consequences for everything we have chosen to believe. As our culture drifts further away from its Judeo-Christian roots, the consequences of what our young people believe are showing up before they reach adulthood.

We don't have to wait until life falls apart to find out whether or not our walk is true. Our emotional response to what we think and believe reveals whether we are on the right path. Remember that our emotions are predominantly a product of our thought life. Consciously or subconsciously, we have certain ideas or goals in our minds for how we should live and what must happen in order for us to be happy, satisfied, and successful. Often, our sense of worth is tied to those goals.

If you found out your supervisor was blocking your goal of being promoted, you would probably feel angry. If the promotion was uncertain, you would probably feel anxious every time you thought about it. If you thought your goal for a promotion was impossible, you would likely feel depressed.

We will be on an emotional roller coaster if we believe our identity and sense of worth are dependent on other people and life's circumstances. If a pastor believes his sense of worth is dependent on the response of his congregation, he may try to manipulate them into responding the way he wants, but every member of the congregation can block that goal. Likewise, if a mother believes her sense of self-worth depends on having a harmonious Christian family, every family member can block that goal, but nobody can keep that mother from being the person God created her to be.

Paul said the goal of our instruction is love (see 1 Timothy 1:5) and "the fruit of the Spirit is love, joy, peace, patience . . . self-control" (Galatians 5:22–23 NASB). Notice the fruit of the Spirit is self-control, not congregational control or child control. Also notice the fruit of the Spirit is singular ("fruit," not "fruits"). God's love manifests itself in joy, peace, and patience. If our goal in life is to become the person God created us to be, then the fruit of the Spirit becomes evident in our lives. Regardless of circumstances, we experience joy instead of depression, peace instead of anxiety, and patience instead of anger. Nobody and nothing can keep us from being sanctified but ourselves.

Why should we consider the long-term consequences of what we choose to believe?

_____

_____

_____

What do anger, anxiety, and depression reveal?

_____

_____

_____

What is fundamentally wrong with people who try to control others or manipulate circumstances in order to meet their goals?

_____

_____

_____

What is keeping you from being the person God created you to be? Is that your goal?

_____

_____

_____

_____

What plans do you have right now that others can block? How can you change that?

_____

_____

_____

His promise is that "my God will supply every need of yours," that God Himself might stand ready to help them receive all that He has provided for them in the abundant greatness of His glory in Christ Jesus. It is indeed the glory of Jesus Christ when by the will of God the desires of Christians are fulfilled in accordance with the teaching of the gospel *(emphasis added).*

Ambrosiaster (written c. AD 366–384)

3

Goals and Desires

Luke 12:13–21

Key Point

There is nothing wrong with having godly desires, but we cannot base our identity and sense of worth on their fulfillment.

Key Verse

It is God's will that you should be sanctified.

1 Thessalonians 4:3

According to Jesus, "life does not consist in the abundance of his possessions" (Luke 12:15). A foolish man works toward the wrong end. To live a successful and satisfied life, we have to have the right goals. No God-given goals for our lives can be impossible, uncertain, or blocked. Even the secular world knows that the authority of leaders is undermined if they issue commands that cannot be obeyed. So, if God wants something done, it can be done! "For nothing will be impossible with God" (Luke 1:37 NASB), and "I can do all things through Christ who strengthens me" (Philippians 4:13 NKJV). However, "all things" has to be consistent with God's will.

To understand how we can successfully live the Christian life, we need to make a distinction between godly goals and godly desires. *A godly goal is any specific orientation that reflects God's purpose for our lives and that is not dependent on people or circumstances beyond our right or ability to control.* The only person we have the right and the ability to control is ourselves. Nobody and nothing can keep us from being the person God created us to be—and God's goal is for us to become that person. If we are honest with ourselves, we will look in the mirror and say, "The only person who can keep me from reaching that goal is me!"

A godly desire is any specific result that depends on the cooperation of other people, the success of events, or favorable circumstances that we have no right or ability to control. We cannot base our identity, success, or sense of worth on our desires, no matter how godly they may be, because we cannot control their fulfillment. God desires that all would repent and live (see Ezekiel 18:32), but not all will. God writes to His children so that they may not sin (see 1 John 2:1), but His sovereignty and His success are not dependent on whether or not we sin.

Suppose a well-meaning pastor has one primary goal, and that is to triple the size of his church and win his community to Christ. Although his desire is a worthy one, every member of the community can block that goal. Relentless in his pursuit, the pastor could start manipulating his people and pressuring them to produce. The pastor's church will suffer a lot of pain until he realizes that his goal is to become the pastor God created him to be, and that this is the best way to reach his community for Christ. If the pastor makes this his primary aim, no one in his congregation can block it. The pastor himself is the only one who can.

There is nothing wrong with having godly desires such as reaching our community for Christ. However, we shouldn't base our identity and sense of worth on their fulfillment. We should never try to control and manipulate people in order to accomplish our goals. Nor should we get angry, anxious, or depressed if our desires are not met—though we may feel disappointed. Life is full of disappointments, but they are likely God's appointments to greater maturity in Christ. Other people don't always cooperate and events don't always go our way, but these realities of life are not keeping us from conforming to the image of God.

In Philippians 4:13, Paul says that we can do all things through Christ. However, what condition must be placed on "all things"?

_____

_____

_____

What is the difference between a godly goal and a godly desire?

_____

_____

_____

Why can we not base our identity or sense of worth on godly desires? What happens when we try to do so?

_____

_____

_____

_____

How can you be the person God created you to be in your profession or role in life?

_____

_____

_____

For the sake of your own emotional stability, what plans/goals do you have right now that should be redefined as a desire?

_____

_____

_____

The good man, being temperate and just, treasures up his wealth in heaven. He who has sold his worldly goods and given them to the poor finds the imperishable treasure "where there is neither moth nor robber." . . . It is not jewels, gold, clothing, or beauty of person that are of high value, but virtue.

Clement of Alexandria (AD 150–215)

4

A True Sense of Worth

2 Peter 1:3–11

Key Point

True believers derive their sense of worth from their identity in Christ and their growth in character.

Key Verses

Therefore, my brothers and sisters, make every effort to confirm your calling and election. For if you do these things, you will never stumble, and you will receive a rich welcome into the eternal kingdom of our Lord and Savior Jesus Christ.

2 Peter 1:10–11

How does a Christian establish a true sense of worth? Some seek for it through the exercise of spiritual gifts! Spiritual gifts are important for building up the Body of Christ, but we don't all have the same gifts. Therefore, "God has put the body together, giving greater honor to the parts that lacked it, so that there should be no division in the body" (1 Corinthians 12:24–25). So, a Christian can't establish worth through spiritual gifts, because those with greater gifts would have greater worth, and that is not true.

Our individual talents make a contribution to the kingdom of God, but God has given five talents to some, two talents to some, and only one talent to others. Does that mean that only the Christian with five talents can have any legitimate sense of worth? The answer is a definite no, and those who try to find their identity and sense of worth in gifts and talents run the risk of not accomplishing God's primary goal for their lives, which is godly character.

Are intelligence, beauty, and performance the means by which we gain a sense of worth? The answer again is no. Paul writes, "God chose the foolish things of the world to shame the wise; God chose the weak things of the world to shame the strong. God chose the lowly things of this world and the despised things—and the things that are not—to nullify the things that are, so that no one may boast before him" (1 Corinthians 1:27–29).

There is certainly nothing wrong with being an intelligent and beautiful performer, especially if you use your gifts to the glory of God. After all, it was God who gave those life endowments! However, while God has not equally distributed gifts, talents, and intelligence to all, He has equally distributed Himself. "His divine power has given us everything we need for a godly life. . . . Through these he has given us his very great and precious promises, so that through them you may participate in the divine nature" (2 Peter 1:3–4).

Unlike this world, the ground before the cross is level. We all have the same standing in Christ. We find our sense of worth in our new identity and in our growth in character. Those who know who they are in Christ and have a life characterized by love, joy, peace, patience, kindness, goodness, faithfulness, gentleness, and self-control will have a legitimate sense of worth and will not be unfruitful. The good news is that every Christian has exactly the same opportunity to accomplish that goal and receive the same inheritance in Christ.

What is wrong if some Christians don't possess these qualities? According to Peter, they have become near-sighted and blind and have lost sight of the fact that they have been cleansed from all their sins (see 2 Peter 1:9). They have taken their eyes off the Lord and have forgotten (or never knew) who they are in Christ. They need to take their eyes off this world and fix their eyes on Jesus, the author and perfecter of their faith. "Dear friends, now we are children of God. . . . All who have this hope in him purify themselves, just as he is pure" (1 John 3:2–3).

What is wrong with basing our sense of worth in God-given endowments rather than in who we are?

_____

_____

_____

How does our relationship with Christ provide us with a sense of worth? Why is this the only legitimate path to feel good about ourselves?

_____

_____

_____

How good would we feel toward ourselves if we failed to grow in character, even if we knew that we are children of God?

_____

_____

_____

How can you have a legitimate sense of worth and never stumble?

_____

_____

_____

If you knew that God loved you as His child and your life demonstrated the fruit of the Spirit, would you feel good about yourself? Why or why not?

There are many who say they have faith in Christ but somehow seem to forget about this pure aspect of it. It is clear that anyone who has real faith will demonstrate that fact by living a life of good works . . . by rejecting ungodliness and worldly desires and by imitating Christ's sober, righteous, and godly life.

Bede (AD 673–735)

5

Righteous Indignation
Mark 11:12–25

Key Point

To be salt and light in this fallen world, we have to speak the truth in love.

Key Verses

"In your anger do not sin": Do not let the sun go down while you are still angry, and do not give the devil a foothold.

Ephesians 4:26–27

A nger is a God-given emotion. We are never instructed to deny our anger, but we are told to manage our emotional life by believing the truth and having the right goals for our lives. The basis for our emotional stability is our identity, acceptance, security, and significance in Christ. Once we are established in Christ, the trials and tribulations of the world no longer have a negative effect on us.

In fact, we "glory in our sufferings, because we know that suffering produces perseverance; perseverance, character; and character, hope. And hope does not put us to shame, because God's love has been poured out into our hearts through the Holy Spirit" (Romans 5:3–5). Trials and tribulations actually reveal wrong goals and make possible the true goal of our lives: conforming to the image of God.

When we think about conforming to God's image, we usually do not think about taking on His righteous wrath. However, the Bible actually talks more about the wrath of God than it does about our wrath. God's anger is not born out of His insecurity, and He doesn't have blocked goals. His anger is a righteous indignation toward sin.

Jesus' cursing of the fig tree and cleansing the Temple illustrate His anger and judgment to come. Jesus didn't get mad because the fig tree had no figs when He wanted some. At that time of the year, the fig tree should have had edible buds—but it did not, which indicated the tree was not going to bear any fruit. The cursing of the fig tree was a prophetic sign of God's impending judgment on Israel, not an angry reaction because Jesus was hungry. The unproductive fig tree symbolized Israel's spiritual barrenness despite their outward appearance of religious fervor.

God's anger is continuous, but His lovingkindness and mercy temper it. God is incredibly patient toward those who sin—we would be much swifter about judging others and forcing them to suffer the consequences. (Remember, Jesus turned over the table, not the moneychangers.) God has the perfect capacity to separate the sin from the sinner. If that were not so, we would all be doomed. We should have a sense of righteous indignation, but we need to learn from His example how to express it.

Abraham Lincoln said, "To sin by silence when they should protest makes cowards of men." Philipp Melanchthon, a contemporary of Martin Luther, said, "All that is needed for sin to abound is for good men to do nothing." Righteous indignation moves us to correct that which is wrong. The heroes of our faith in Hebrews 11 could not sit by and watch the world go to hell. They had to do something, even if it cost them their lives—and it often did.

If we are going to be salt and light in this fallen world, we need to speak the truth, but we need to do it in love. We must make a stand for righteousness, but we should silently stand by if we can't do so without violating the fruit of the Spirit. To speak the truth without love would make us no different from those who represent the ideals we are standing against—and it would profit no one. Let the message spoken in love—not the messenger—be the offense.

How can we be angry but not sin?

_____

_____

_____

_____

Knowing that hope is the present assurance of some future good, why can we glory in our sufferings? How does that help us persevere?

_____

_____

_____

_____

In Mark 11:12–25, why did Jesus curse the fig tree?

_____

_____

_____

Why do you suppose God created you to experience anger as an emotion?

_____

_____

_____

_____

What righteous stand do you need to make at work, home, or in the world?

> *Suffering is the measure of how much hope we have, and it testifies to the fact that we deserve the crown we shall inherit. This is why the Lord said, "Blessed are you when they persecute you and say all kinds of evil things against you on account of God's righteousness. Rejoice and be glad, for your reward will be great." For to despise present sufferings and hindrances, and for the hope of the future, not to give in to pressure has great merit with God.*
>
> Ambrosiaster (written c. AD 366–384)

Who Is Responsible for What?

Paul said that God would strengthen and protect us from the evil one (see 2 Thessalonians 3:3). Then he continues by saying we ought to carry out our own responsibilities and not become idle. In God's mind, there is a clear line between His sovereignty and our responsibility.

God's sovereignty | Our responsibility

On the left side is what God and only God can do. If we try to usurp the role of God, we will invariably become frustrated and fail. We are not God. We can't even save ourselves. We should not try to be someone else's conscience, and we cannot change another person. Nothing will interfere with Christian relationships and ministry more than attempting to play the role of God in another person's life. The key is to know God and His ways and live accordingly. That way, we won't be disappointed when He doesn't respond the way we wanted Him to respond.

The right side of the line depicts our responsibility. God will not do for us what He has commanded us to do. God can only do that which is consistent with His nature and His Word. God cannot lie, and He will not change to accommodate us. We can't ask God to study His Word for us when He commanded us to study it (see 2 Timothy 2:15). God will enable us to do all that He has commanded, but He will not believe for us, forgive others for us, repent for us, or assume any of our responsibilities that He has delegated to us.

Not recognizing who is responsible for what is devastating when it comes to resolving spiritual conflicts. Suppose people are terrified of a spiritual presence in their room. They pull the covers over their heads and cry out, "God, do something!" But God doesn't seem to do anything. So they wonder, *Why don't you help me, God? You are all powerful. You can make it go away. Maybe You don't care, or maybe I'm not a Christian. Maybe that is why You're not helping!* People question God's love, His presence in their lives, and their salvation when they don't know who is responsible for what.

God *did* do something. He disarmed the devil, made us new creations in Christ, and seated us with Him in the heavenlies. He has given us the authority and the responsibility to resist the devil. We also have the responsibility to put on the armor of God and take every thought captive and make it obedient to Christ. However, what will happen if we don't assume our responsibility?

Overcoming Anxiety

T here are two days in every week about which we should not worry—two days that should be kept free from fear and apprehension. One of those days is *yesterday,* with its mistakes and cares, faults and blunders, and aches and pains. Yesterday has passed forever beyond our control, and all the money in the world cannot bring it back. We cannot undo a single act we performed or erase a single word we said. Yesterday is gone.

The other day we should not worry about is *tomorrow*, with its possible adversaries, its burdens, and its large promise and poor performance. Tomorrow is also beyond our immediate control. Tomorrow's sun will rise either in splendor or behind a mask of clouds . . . but it will rise. Until it does, we have no stake in tomorrow, for it is yet unborn.

That leaves only one day . . . *today*. Any person can fight the battles of just one day; it is only when you add the burdens of those two awful eternities—yesterday and tomorrow—that we break down.

It is not the experience of today that drives us mad. It is remorse or bitterness for something that happened yesterday and the dread of what tomorrow may bring.

Daily Readings

1. Dealing With Worry	Matthew 6:19–34
2. Double-Minded Thinking	Joshua 24:14–28
3. "Plan A" Living	Mark 7:1–9
4. Knowing God's Ways	Jeremiah 9:1–26
5. Casting Our Anxieties on Christ	1 Peter 5:6–10

1

Dealing With Worry

Matthew 6:19–34

Key Point

There is no need to be anxious about God's providential care if we seek Him first.

Key Verses

But seek first his kingdom and his righteousness, and all these things will be given to you as well. Therefore do not worry about tomorrow, for tomorrow will worry about itself.

Matthew 6:33–34

In the Sermon on the Mount, Jesus teaches that anxious people have two treasures and two visions, because they try to serve two masters. Such double-minded people inevitably worry about tomorrow and their possessions. Regarding the latter, there is the constant concern for maintaining and protecting material possessions. The second law of thermodynamics (the law of entropy) states that without the introduction of new energy, all systems become progressively more disorderly and will decay. If rust doesn't destroy them, then moths or termites will. Earthly treasures tempt other people to covet and steal, which will pose a concern for their security. It is hard to be anxiety-free when we are worried about our possessions.

It is important to note that there is nothing inherently wrong with having material possessions. It is the love of money—not money itself—that is the root of all sorts of evil (see 1 Timothy 6:10). Paul tells us, "Command those who are rich in this present world not to be arrogant nor to put their hope in wealth, which is so uncertain, but to put their hope in God, who richly provides us with everything for our enjoyment. Command them to do good, to be rich in good deeds, and to be generous and willing to share. In this way they will lay up treasure for themselves as a firm foundation for the coming age, so that they may take hold of the life that is truly life" (verses 17–19). Personal security comes from relationships, not physical possessions. The critical question is what do we treasure in our hearts. There will be no peace trying to serve two masters. Whichever master we choose to serve, by that master we shall be controlled.

Jesus then addresses the matter of our provision. People are anxious about tomorrow because they don't know what tomorrow brings. Trusting God for tomorrow is a question of our worth. Birds are not created in the image of God, but we are! Birds will not inherit the kingdom of God, but we will! If God takes care of the birds, how much more will He take care of us! "If . . . God clothes the grass of the field, which is here today and tomorrow is thrown into the fire, will he not much more clothe you?" (Matthew 6:30).

God lays His own reputation on the line. It is our responsibility to trust and obey. It is His responsibility to remain faithful. This is a question of God's integrity. Does He care for you, and will He provide for your needs? Yes and yes! Your heavenly Father knows what you need. "Therefore do not worry about tomorrow, for tomorrow will worry about itself. Each day has enough trouble of its own" (verse 34).

Do you believe that the fruit of the Spirit will satisfy you more than earthly possessions? Do you believe that if you hunger and thirst after righteousness you will be satisfied? Do you believe that God will supply all your needs according to His riches in glory? If you do, then you will "seek first his kingdom and his righteousness, and all these things will be given to you as well" (verse 33).

What is the problem with being double-minded?

_____

_____

_____

Why do people worry about their possessions?

_____

_____

_____

What is the difference between the security people hope to gain with material possessions and the security Christians can have in righteous relationships with God and each other?

_____

_____

_____

What are you worried about? Whose responsibility is it?

_____

_____

_____

What do you treasure in your heart? Which master are you serving?

_____

_____

_____

Do you see how Jesus clarifies what has been obscure by comparing it to what is self-evident? Can you add one cubit, or even the slightest measure, to your bodily life span by worrying about it? Can you by being anxious about food add moments to your life? Hence it is clear that it is not our diligence but the providence of God, even where we seem to be active, that finally accompanies everything. In the light of God's providence, none of our cares, anxieties, toils or any other such things will ever come to anything, but will utterly pass away.

John Chrysostom (AD 347–407)

2

Double-Minded Thinking
Joshua 24:14–28

Key Point

The mind that is focused on Christ is anxious-free.

Key Verses

You must believe and not doubt, because the one who doubts is like a wave of the sea, blown and tossed by the wind. . . . Such a person is double-minded and unstable in all they do.

James 1:6, 8

In the New Testament, the primary words for anxiety are the noun *merimna* and the verb *merimnao*. Of the 25 uses, 5 indicate a sense of caring, while the other 20 refer to a distracting, negative sense of worry or dread. In the positive sense, we should feel anxious if we have an important responsibility to fulfill, and it should motivate us to take necessary steps to carry out our responsibility. Most of our anxious thoughts, however, are not profitable and can lead to psychosomatic illnesses.

Worrying doesn't accomplish anything and won't prevent something from happening. We are not going to help the plane stay in the air by worrying, and we are not going to improve the odds in our favor by fretting about all that could go wrong. Jesus says, "Can any one of you by worrying add a single hour to your life?" (Matthew 6:27). On the other hand, excessive worrying can take some years off our lives.

Remember that anxiety differs from fear in that fear has an object whereas anxiety doesn't. We are anxious because our future is uncertain and we don't know what is going to happen tomorrow. This process of worrying can be more debilitating than actually experiencing the negative consequences of what we worried about. In fact, some of us feel relieved to have the anxious "waiting" period over, even if the much worried over "happening" hasn't turned out the way we wanted.

It is easier for us to live with "what is" than it is to live with "what if." When we don't know what is going to happen tomorrow, we are tempted to make assumptions. It seems to be a peculiar trait of our minds to assume the worst. However, nothing good can come from making negative assumptions and then acting on them as though they were facts.

The root of *merimna* is the verb *merizo*, which means "to draw in different directions or distract." When *merimna* is used as a verb (*merimnao*), it appears to be a conjunction of *merizo* and *nous*, which means mind. That is probably why the translators of the *King James Version* translated "do not worry" (Matthew 6:25) as "take no thought," and "why do you worry" (Matthew 6:28) as "why take ye thought."

To be anxious in a negative sense is to be double-minded, and James says a double-minded person is unstable in all their ways (see James 1:8). This is clearly revealed in Jesus' words in Matthew 6:24–25: "No one can serve two masters. Either you will hate the one and love the other, or you will be devoted to the one and despise the other. You cannot serve both God and money. Therefore I tell you, do not worry about your life."

When Joshua gave his farewell address, the Israelites had yet to fully possess the land and had many more battles to fight. So Joshua, knowing that his leaving might create uncertainties in their minds, reminded them of how the Lord had delivered them and advised them, "Fear the Lord and serve him with all faithfulness. . . . But if serving the Lord seems undesirable to you, then choose for yourselves this day whom you will serve. . . . But as for me and my household, we will serve the LORD" (Joshua 24:14–15).

When is anxiousness a postive feedback? When is it negative?

_____

_____

_____

_____

Why is it easier to deal with what is than what might be?

_____

_____

_____

In what ways does anxiety reveal that we are attempting to serve two masters?

_____

_____

_____

_____

How can you turn a negative state of mind into a positive one?

_____

_____

_____

_____

What kind of assumptions do you naturally make when you are anxious about something?

A man is double-minded when he wants to have fun in this world but also reign with God in heaven. Likewise, a man is double-minded when he seeks the approval of others for his good deeds rather than spiritual rewards from God.

Bede (AD 673–735)

3

"Plan A" Living

Mark 7:1–9

Key Point

Our emotional stability and lifestyle will reveal which plan we have chosen to follow.

Key Verse

Whether you turn to the right or to the left, your ears will hear a voice behind you, saying, "This is the way; walk in it."

Isaiah 30:21

To overcome anxiety, we need to acquire a singleness of vision and purpose. The question is whether we are going to live *our* way or *God's* way. Let's call God's way "Plan A," which we accept by faith, and humanity's way "Plan B," which is a natural product of human reason and intuition. There are times when God's ways don't make sense to us because we don't have the big picture. Because of our limited human perspective we can never know if we are basing our decisions on all the facts, and we can't predict what the consequences of our actions will be. That is why God says His ways are not our ways (see Isaiah 55:8).

When we come to Christ, our old ways of thinking and living are still programmed into our minds. If we don't know God's ways, we will continue to live the way we always have. Now that we have the mind of Christ (see 1 Corinthians 2:16), we can learn God's ways. However, until we are fully committed to living according to what God says is true, we will waffle between Plan A and Plan B.

When we commit ourselves to live according to God's way (Plan A), it decreases our tendency to live as we always have (Plan B). When we mix our ways with God's ways, it decreases our commitment to Plan A. That is what the Pharisees were doing by observing their man-made traditions (Plan B), and as a result they set aside the commandments of God (Plan A). Such waffling creates anxieties for us as Christians because we are double-minded.

The unbeliever can experience less anxiety than an immature or uncommitted Christian who straddles the fence in order to have the "best" of both worlds. The natural person creates his or her own rationalistic worldview and explanation of reality and can live anxiety-free in this world for a time. The natural person has become his or her own god. However, "There is a way that appears to be right, but in the end it leads to death" (Proverbs 14:12). We can't choose Plan B just because it seems less worrisome in the present. Satan will always tempt us with an alternative to Plan A that may seem right to the non-discerning, but it leads to certain destruction.

To illustrate this principle, consider marriage. God's Plan A for marriage is a life-long monogamous relationship between a man and a woman, for better or for worse, until death separates them. We should never entertain thoughts contrary to that commitment, because that will be the temptation that leads to divorce. Thinking what it would be like to be married to someone else is pure fantasy, which will appear more attractive than the reality we have.

What would happen if a young couple got married with the understanding that they could always get a divorce if the relationship didn't work out? They *will* probably get divorced, because commitment is what makes the marriage relationship unique. If a wife establishes her own career because she believes the marriage won't last, she is making preparations for Plan B. If a husband is more committed to his job than his marriage, he is choosing Plan B. Your emotional stability and lifestyle will reveal which plan you have chosen.

What two limitations do we have when charting our own course of action?

Why do believers still waffle between trying to follow their ways and God's ways after they receive new life in Christ?

Why does the natural person often experience less anxiety than an immature or uncommitted Christian who is "straddling the fence"?

Where do you experience the most tension between your old ways and God's ways?

Why is it foolish to make your own provisions in case Plan A doesn't work? Isn't that doubting God?

_____

_____

_____

They [the Pharisees] enjoined an adulterated law at cross-purposes with the divine law. The Lord made this clear when He asked them: "Why do you transgress God's commandments for the sake of your traditions?" By their transgression they not only falsified God's law . . . but they also set against it their own law, called this day the Pharisaic law. In this their rabbis suppress some of the commandments, add new ones, and give others their own interpretation, thus making the law serve their own purposes.

Irenaeus (AD 130–202)

4

Knowing God's Ways

Jeremiah 9:1–26

Key Point

Peace comes when we live in harmony with the God-created rhythms of life.

Key Verse

Let the one who boasts boast in the Lord.

1 Corinthians 1:31

Someone speculated that every decision people make is an attempt to reduce further anxiety. To cope with anxiety, people consume food, alcohol, and drugs; have illicit sex; mindlessly repeat mantras; and escape to cabins, boats, and lonely places. More prescription drugs are dispensed for the temporary "cure" of anxiety than for any other reason. But when the temporary cures wear off, we have to return to the same world—only now we have the added problem of the negative consequences of the escape mechanisms. Anxiety drains our energy today and dims our hope for tomorrow.

97

Anxiety arises out of a state of disconnection. Human wisdom, strength, and riches cannot comprehend, accomplish, or buy the peace that comes from being rightly related to God. The only thing we can boast about is our understanding of God and His ways (see Jeremiah 9:23–24). God has designed us to live a certain way, and living any other way is like swimming upstream in our own strength or succumbing to the current and being swept helplessly along. Having the peace of God regardless of external circumstances is like floating on a pond.

Life is like a factory that has hundreds of gears all intertwined and running together. It runs smoothly as long as the gears are well oiled and perfectly centered. Should one of the gears get a little out-of-round and start taking an elliptical path, it will no longer mesh with the other gears and will quickly wear out. The out-of-place gear not only does damage to itself but also creates friction with those gears closely connected to it. In the same way, we have to stay closely connected to God and to our fellow believers if we are to become the people God wants us to be.

However, we can't work together as a harmonious whole unless we are Christ-centered and submissive to His ways. We need to discover the God-created harmony and rhythms of life. He is the Master Musician, and we are His orchestra. When we are filled with His Spirit, we will sing and make melody in our hearts to the Lord (see Ephesians 5:19). If each of us follows the Director and plays our part, the music will be a glorious expression of His glory. But if our timing is off, or if we play a different tune, we create an awful noise. To go to the grave with our music still in us would be the greatest tragedy of all.

In the time of Jeremiah, the Israelites were not living in harmony with God. Jeremiah was disgusted with these unfaithful people and wanted to get away from them (see Jeremiah 9:2). They were self-centered and had not followed God's ways (see verses 13–14). Their attempt to correct their own problems was at best superficial. "They dress the wounds of my people as though it were not serious. 'Peace, peace,' they say, when there is no peace" (8:11).

God never gives bandage-answers to cancerous problems. He said to the people, "Let not the wise boast of their wisdom or the strong boast of their strength or the rich man boast of their riches, but let the one who boasts boast about this: that they have the understanding to know me, that I am the LORD, who exercises kindness, justice and righteousness on earth, for in these I delight" (9:23–24).

What are some of the temporal cures for anxiety? Why are they ineffective?

_____

_____

_____

_____

Why do we need to be Christ-centered if we want to be anxious-free?

_____

_____

_____

_____

Why does world peace keep eluding us?

_____

_____

_____

_____

To what or whom have you turned when feeling anxious?

_____

_____

_____

How can you become single-minded when feeling anxious?

_____

_____

_____

*It is part of those who have been perfected not to be easily influ-
enced by worldly things or to be troubled with fear or tormented
with suspicion or stunned with dread or distressed with pain.
Rather, as if on a shore of total safety, they ought to calm their
spirit, immoveable as it is in the anchorage of faith against the
rising waves and tempests of the world. Christ brought this
support to the spirits of Christians when He brought an inner
peace to the souls of those who had proved themselves, so that
our heart should not be troubled or our spirit be distressed.*

Ambrose (AD 340–397)

5

Casting Our Anxieties
on Christ

1 Peter 5:6–10

Key Point

We overcome anxiety by surrendering our ways and submitting to God's ways.

Key Verse

The fruit of that righteousness will be peace.

Isaiah 32:17

C hrist has invited you to cast your anxieties on Him, because He cares for you. This means that you have to humble yourself by surrendering your ways and submitting to His ways. The following steps will help you overcome anxiety.

First, before you do anything else, you should pray. Paul writes, "Do not be anxious about anything, but in every situation, by prayer and petition, with thanksgiving, present your requests to God" (Philippians 4:6). Pray,

"Lord, I come humbly before Your presence as Your child. I acknowledge my dependence on You, and I ask for Your divine guidance. Show me what I am responsible for and what I am not. Fill me with Your Holy Spirit and guide me into all truth. I ask for Your peace to guard my heart and my mind in Christ Jesus. Amen."

Second, resolve all personal and spiritual conflicts by submitting to God and resisting the devil. "Submit yourselves, then, to God. Resist the devil, and he will flee from you" (James 4:7). You do this through genuine repentance (see the Steps to Freedom in Christ). The purpose is to make sure your heart is right with God and to eliminate any demonic influences on your mind.

Third, state the problem. What are you anxious about? A problem well stated is half solved. In anxious states of mind, people can't see the forest for the trees. So put the problem in perspective. What matters for eternity? Seek godly counsel if necessary, but do not turn to ungodly counsel or temporary cures.

Fourth, separate the facts from the assumptions. People are not anxious about what they know; they are anxious about what they *don't* know. People may be fearful of the facts, but not anxious.

Fifth, determine what you have the right or the ability to control. Remember that your duty in life and your sense of worth are tied only to that for which you are responsible. If you aren't living a responsible life, you should feel anxious. Don't try to cast your responsibility on Christ, for He will just throw it back. However, do cast your anxiety onto Him, because His integrity is at stake in meeting your needs—if you are living a responsible and righteous life.

Sixth, list everything you can do that is related to the situation that is under your responsibility. What is the noble thing to do? How can you assume your responsibility in a dignified manner that is worthy of respect? What is the right thing to do? What is the morally pure thing to do? What could you do that would promote peace and goodwill? What could you do that would be positive and constructive rather than negative and destructive?

Seventh, complete everything on your list. Commit yourself to be a responsible person and fulfill your calling and obligations in life. Take every thought captive in obedience to Christ and keep your mind focused on what is true.

Finally, submit to God in prayer everything that lies outside of your responsibility and your right or ability to control. If you have fulfilled your responsibilities and believe the truth, the rest is God's responsibility. Any residual anxiety is probably due to your having assumed responsibilities that God never intended you to have.

If the Steps to Freedom in Christ are not available, ask the Lord to reveal to your mind any sin that is keeping you from having an intimate relationship with Him. Write those in the space below.

State specifically what you are anxious about, and separate the facts from the assumptions.

Determine what you have the right and the ability to control and commit yourself to accomplish what you are responsible for.

Write down how you can assist others who are directly connected to the situation in question with their responsibility without usurping their role. Commit the rest to God in prayer.

_____

_____

_____

Peace, indeed, is serenity of mind, tranquility of soul, simplicity of heart, the bond of love, the fellowship of charity. It removes hatred, settles wars, restrains wrath, tramples on pride, loves the humble, pacifies the discordant and makes enemies agree. For it is pleasing to everyone. It does not seek what belongs to another or consider anything its own. It teaches people to love because it does not get angry, or to extol itself or become inflated with pride. It is meek and humble to everyone, possessing rest and tranquility within itself. When the peace of Christ is exercised by a Christian, it is brought to perfection by Christ.

Caesarius of Arles (AD 470–542)

Assuming Our Responsibility

James 5:13–16 is one place in the Bible that specifically says what we are supposed to do if we are sick or suffering. The tendency is to focus on the role of the elders, while the responsibilities of the suffering and sick are overlooked. The prayer of a righteous elder will not be effective if the person in trouble is not assuming his or her responsibility. There are three reasons for this.

First, we cannot do other people's praying for them. Initially, the one who is suffering is the one who should be praying (see verse 13). Intercessory

104

prayer is never intended to replace another person's responsibility to pray. Christians don't function as mediums. There is only "one mediator between God and mankind, the man Jesus Christ" (1 Timothy 2:5). If you had a daughter who kept coming to you on behalf of your son, wouldn't you tell your daughter to advise her brother to come see you personally? We cannot have a secondhand relationship with God. Every child of God has the same access to Him. The only effective prayer at this stage is the prayer of a repentant heart. If we cherish sin in our hearts, the Lord will not hear us (see Psalm 66:18). The answer is to deal with the sin, not ask someone else to do our praying for us.

Second, God puts the responsibility on those who are suffering and sick to take the initiative to call the elders (see James 5:14). We should help one another, but we can't assume their responsibility for them. Any lasting change for good in their lives will be directly related to what they have chosen to believe and do in response to God, not to what others do. Those who are looking for someone to fix them will never get fixed.

Third, confession, which is open and honest agreement with God, must come before healing (see verse 16). All too often elders are summoned to pray for the sick, only to discover later that those for whom they prayed are living in bondage to sin, bitterness, pride, and rebellion. The loving thing to do is to help them resolve their personal and spiritual conflicts by submitting to God and resisting the devil. If those who are sick and suffering for spiritual and psychosomatic reasons will truly repent, then the prayers of the righteous will be effective. We can't expect God to bless and heal those who are rebelling against Him and His ways.

Overcoming Depression

The pain is unrelenting, and what makes the condition intolerable is the foreknowledge that no remedy will come—not in a day, an hour, a month, or a minute. If there is mild relief, one knows that it is only temporary; more pain will follow. It is hopelessness even more than the pain that crushes the soul. So the decision-making of daily life involves not, as in normal affairs, shifting from one annoying situation to another less annoying—of from discomfort to relative comfort, or from boredom to activity—but moving from pain to pain. One does not abandon even briefly, one's bed of nails, but is attached to it wherever one goes.

—Novelist William Styron in *The Darkness Visible*[2]

Daily Readings

1. Diagnosing Depression	Psalm 38:1–22
2. The Basis for Our Hope	Psalm 13:1–6
3. Overcoming Hopelessness	Hebrews 6:13–19
4. The Problem of Helplessness	Exodus 6:6–12
5. Overcoming Helplessness	Numbers 13:26–14:9

1

Diagnosing Depression
Psalm 38:1–22

Key Point

Taking a pill to cure your body is commendable, but taking a pill to cure your soul is deplorable.

Key Verse

Hope deferred makes the heart sick, but a longing fulfilled is a tree of life.

Proverbs 13:12

Every population group is experiencing a blues epidemic in this age of anxiety. The number of people seeking medical treatment for depression has doubled during the last decade. Depression is often called the "common cold of mental illness," because it is so prevalent. Like anxiety disorders, depression arises out of a state of disconnection from God. After the Fall, Adam was fearful and anxious (see Genesis 3:10), while Cain, his son, was angry and depressed (see Genesis 4:5). Depression is often the response to losses in our lives, and humankind's greatest loss has been our relationship with God.

In Psalm 38, David records nearly every symptom of depression. In verses 1 through 8 he reveals the suffering of separation, and in verses 9 through 14 he reveals the loneliness of separation. Depression is a sense of helplessness and hopelessness, and David wisely turns to the God of hope and help (see verse 22). Determine your state of depression by circling the numbers that best represents you in the following symptom scale (1 for very low energy and 5 for very high energy):

1. Low energy	1	2	3	4	5	High energy
2. Difficulty sleeping/sleep all the time	1	2	3	4	5	Uninterrupted sleeping patterns
3. No desire to be involved in activities	1	2	3	4	5	Very involved in activities
4. No desire for sex	1	2	3	4	5	Healthy sex drive
5. Aches and pains	1	2	3	4	5	Feel great
6. Loss of appetite	1	2	3	4	5	Enjoy eating
7. Sad (tearful)	1	2	3	4	5	Joyful
8. Despairing and hopeless	1	2	3	4	5	Hopeful and confident
9. Irritable (low frustration tolerance)	1	2	3	4	5	Pleasant (high frustration tolerance)
10. Withdrawn	1	2	3	4	5	Involved
11. Mental anguish	1	2	3	4	5	Peace of mind
12. Low sense of self-worth	1	2	3	4	5	High sense of self-worth
13. Pessimistic about the future	1	2	3	4	5	Optimistic about the future
14. Perceive most circumstances as negative and harmful to self	1	2	3	4	5	Perceive most circumstances as positive and as opportunities for growth
15. Self-destructive (myself and others would be better if I weren't here)	1	2	3	4	5	Self-preserving (I'm glad I'm here)

If you circled mostly ones and twos, you are *severely depressed*. If you circled mostly twos, you are *depressed*. If you circled mostly twos and threes, you are *mildly depressed*. Note that depression affects your body, soul, and spirit, and recovery requires a wholistic answer. There are biological and neurological causes for depression that you should consider in order to have a comprehensive answer. In such cases, medication may be necessary. However, most causes of depression are psychological and spiritual. Medical doctors and Christian caregivers need to work together in order to provide a complete answer. Taking a pill to cure your body is commendable, but taking a pill to cure your soul is deplorable. May God give you the wisdom to know the difference.

Why do you think so many people today suffer from depression?

Why do you think that 50 percent of those suffering from depression never seek treatment?

Why should we consider treatments other than drugs for depression?

What did you learn about yourself from the symptom scale?

_____

_____

_____

Do you think depression is a sin and taking medicine shows a lack of faith? Explain.

_____

_____

_____

"Sing with jubilation to God, all the earth." The prophet was troubled for the faithful people in case they believe they are to serve the Lord with gloomy anxiety, so he began at once with jubilation, for ministering to the Lord with happiness of mind constitutes the perfect devotion of the just man. As Paul warns us, "Always rejoice; pray without ceasing; in all things give thanks."

Cassiodorus (AD 490–585)

2

The Basis for Our Hope

Psalm 13:1–6

Key Point

Hope is the present assurance of some future good.

Key Verse

Why, my soul, are you downcast? Why so disturbed within me? Put your hope in God, for I will yet praise him, my Savior and my God.

Psalm 42:5

American sociologist Lewis Mumford once said, "Without food man can survive for barely 30 days; without water for little more than 3 days; without air hardly for more than 3 minutes: but without hope he might destroy himself in an even shorter time."[1] Hope is not wishful thinking; it is the present assurance of some future good. Depression is a sense of hopelessness born out of a negative and often false perception of ourselves, our circumstances, and the future. The resulting emotional state may not be based on reality nor perceived truthfully from God's

113

perspective. Remember that if what we believe does not reflect truth, then what we feel does not reflect reality.

In Psalm 13, David exhibits many of the classic symptoms of depression including hopelessness, negative self-talk, thoughts of death, and sadness. David is depressed because he is focusing on his circumstances, sees no future hope, and has a false perception of himself and God. Even though he believes in God, he is depressed, because what he believes about God is not true. How can an omnipresent and omniscient God forget him for even one minute, much less forever? Depressed people often have a distorted concept of God and of themselves. If you believe that God has forgotten you, then you have no hope. If you think you have lost your salvation or never had it, then you have no hope.

David's wrestling with his thoughts (see Psalm 13:2) is the endless rumination of self-talk. There is no answer in that squirrel cage. Turning to God is the answer, and that is what David does (see Psalm 13:5–6). So does the oppressed psalmist when he repeats the following verse three times: "Why, my soul, are you downcast? Why so disturbed within me? Put your hope in God, for I will yet praise him, my Savior and my God" (Psalms 42:5, 11; 43:5).

David overcomes his depression in three ways. First, he places his trust in God's unfailing love (see Psalm 13:5). He had always trusted in God, but he had allowed his negative circumstances to draw his attention away from the Lord. The light of God's eternal love illuminates his dark, temporal, and fleeting circumstances. God is the only constant in this ever-changing world.

Second, David's heart rejoices in his salvation. He remembers that he has a covenant relationship with God—and so do we. God hasn't changed, and His Word hasn't changed (see 1 John 3:2–3). When we find our hope fading, we should recall again who God is and who we are in Christ.

Third, David sings to the Lord. Singing is one of the key ways to focus our minds. One of the main determinants of whether a depressed mood will persist or lift is the degree to which we ruminate. Worrying about what is depressing us makes the depression more intense and prolonged. Singing hymns of praise can help us stop wrestling with our thoughts, and it is something we can choose to do. There is also a spiritual dimension of music we shouldn't overlook. When David played the harp, the evil spirit departed from Saul (see 1 Samuel 16:21–23), and the hand of the Lord came on Elisha when the harpist played (see 2 Kings 3:15). Martin Luther also struggled with depression and wrote the classic hymn "A Mighty Fortress Is Our God."

How can the present assurance of some future good help the depressed person?

In Psalm 13, what are some of the symptoms of depression that David exhibits? In what ways is David's concept of himself and God distorted?

In what three ways does David overcome his depression?

How can a true knowledge of God and a true understanding of who you are "in Christ" be a defense against depression?

What can you do when you find yourself caught in negative self-talk?

_____

_____

_____

We shall see Him [Jesus] as He is, because we shall be like Him. This is our hope for the future, our love in the present and our faith in both the past and the present.

Hilary of Arles (AD 403–449)

3

Overcoming Hopelessness

Hebrews 6:13–19

Key Point

Proven character is hope realized.

Key Verse

We have this hope as an anchor for the soul, firm and secure.

Hebrews 6:19

There was a man who was abruptly awakened by a bright light in his room. The heavenly encounter was accompanied with a clear impression on his mind. When he woke up the next morning, he knew what his calling was. He had to speak out against the slaughter of unborn children. The task was formidable. Many states had laws that needed to be overturned, but that seemed unlikely since the Supreme Court had legalized abortion. The liberal press favored the "rights" of mothers to abort their children. So where should he start?

First, he needed to educate himself. So he read volumes about reproduction and medical ethics. He wrote letters to the editors of magazines and newspapers. He worked to elect local politicians who shared his views. He marched for pro-life and picketed abortion clinics. He worked tirelessly for years, but he grew more and more disillusioned with his progress. He fought off bitterness against his perceived adversaries and the flaming darts of the enemy, who was relentless.

Look at your feeble efforts, the devil said. *You're not accomplishing anything. So why don't you quit and have a little fun in life!* The devil's advice was tempting, but the man took his case to the Lord one night. "God," he said, "I feel like a failure. I am so discouraged. I wanted to please you, but nothing seems to have changed." In the stillness of night, another heavenly impression came to his mind. *My child, I asked you to speak out against abortion, and this you have done. You have renewed your mind, learned how to speak the truth in love, and put on the armor of God. You are more patient, kind, and loving than you were before, and yet you feel hopeless because you have not impacted the laws of the land or stopped the press of the ungodly. I never asked you to do that. I, my child, will "convict the world of guilt in regard to sin and righteousness and judgment."*

If you want to feel discouraged and depressed, try assuming God's responsibility for Him. In this world we are going to face negative circumstances and inevitable losses. Suffering is part of our sanctification. "We boast in the hope of the glory of God. Not only so, but we also glory in our sufferings, because we know that suffering produces perseverance; perseverance, character; and character, hope. And hope does not put us to shame, because God's love has been poured out into our hearts through the Holy Spirit" (Romans 5:2–5).

This job seems hopeless, so I think I will change jobs. This marriage seems hopeless, so I think I will dump this one and look for another spouse. Such are the musings of the hopeless. There may be times when we need to change jobs and move, but in many cases what we really need to do is hang in there and grow up! We only make matters worse if we keep running away from the lessons of life.

"Consider it pure joy, my brothers and sisters, whenever you face trials of many kinds, because you know that the testing of your faith develops perseverance. Let perseverance finish its work so that you may be mature and complete, not lacking anything" (James 1:2–4). This is not Christian masochism. This is how we can have proven character—and that is the basis for our hope in God.

Why do some get discouraged serving God and standing for righteousness?

Why is it so important that we know who is responsible for what? What are some of the consequences if we don't?

Is a Christian ever hopeless? Why or why not?

What causes you to be discouraged in serving God?

How can you avoid becoming depressed over a seeming lack of progress?

_____

_____

_____

Nobody will take the disciples' joy from them because, although they suffered persecution and torture on behalf of Christ's name, yet they willingly bore all adversities because they were enkindled by hope in His resurrection and by their vision of Him. Moreover, they thought it perfect joy when they encountered different kinds of temptations.

Bede (AD 673–735)

4

The Problem of Helplessness
Exodus 6:6–12

Key Point

The Lord is our ever present help in time of need.

Key Verse

When he saw the crowds, he had compassion on them, because they were harassed and helpless, like sheep without a shepherd.

Matthew 9:36

Human beings, endowed by the Creator with mental and physical powers, have launched satellites into space. They have transplanted hearts, kidneys, and livers, allowing people to live longer. They have climbed the highest peaks, descended into the lowest depths, and probed the universe, going where no one has gone before. Athletes keep chopping inches and seconds off world records.

However, there is a limit to what finite humans can do. If we were gods—as the false prophets of the New Age movement would have us believe—there would be no limit to what we could do. But we are not gods, and without God we will eventually find ourselves in a helpless situation. Our finite resources can help us overcome many obstacles for a time, but in the end they cannot save us.

Helplessness is a primary symptom of depression, and often it is learned. Take fleas, for instance. If you put them in a beaker with a glass plate over the top, after a few attempts to fly out, they will remain in the beaker even after you remove the glass plate. If you put a glass divider in an aquarium with a fish on one side and its favorite food on the other, within a few days the fish will remain on its side after you remove the divider. Baby elephants that are chained to a stake in the ground will remain staked to the ground even when they are older and can easily pull up the stake.

This all occurs because they learned to be helpless when they were young. The Israelites suffered from a similar kind of helplessness. They couldn't believe good news when they heard it! God instructed Moses to tell the Israelites that He would bring them out of slavery in Egypt and be their God (see Exodus 6:6–7). When Moses shared this with the Israelites, they didn't listen to him, "because of their discouragement and harsh labor" (verse 9). Years of conditioning had left them with a sense of helplessness. Even Moses felt helpless to persuade Pharaoh, for he had learned by experience that he could not even persuade his own people. It is not uncommon today to see entire people groups gripped by depression because they feel helpless to change their circumstances.

Scientific experiments show that a real or perceived sense of helplessness affects our neurochemistry. Helping people overcome their sense of helplessness and hopelessness has proven to be as effective as antidepressant medication—without the potentially negative side effects. So, if the precipitating cause for depression is not neurological, should we take medication? Perhaps the question is best answered by an analogy. If we are suffering from acid indigestion, should we take an antacid? Yes, but that is not a complete answer. We should probably consider changing our eating habits and investigate other potential causes for the upset stomach, such as ulcers or cancer.

Why has there been a tenfold increase in depression during the last 50 years? It is doubtful that our brain chemistry or our genes have changed radically. The problem lies more with what we believe and how we live. Our hope has been misplaced, our beliefs have strayed from the truth, and we have failed to learn how we can overcome helplessness by turning to God.

How is depression a symptom of helplessness? In what ways is it a learned trait?

_____

_____

_____

According to Exodus 6:6–9, why did the Israelites have trouble believing Moses?

_____

_____

_____

What are the many ways that we truly are helpless without God?

_____

_____

_____

Where and when do you feel helpless? How can you change that perception?

_____

_____

_____

Why do you think the whole world is experiencing a "blues" epidemic?

....

....

....

No instigator had stirred up the crowds. They were not harassed and helpless because of some mishap or disturbance. So why was Jesus so moved with compassion [Matthew 9:36] for these people? Clearly the Lord has pity on these people held in the sway of an unclean spirit and burdened by the law, because no shepherd was about to restore to them the guardianship of the Holy Spirit.

Hilary of Arles (AD 403–449)

5

Overcoming Helplessness

Numbers 13:26–14:9

Key Point

Helplessness is overcome through the power of God and by believing His truth.

Key Verse

I can do all this through him who gives me strength.

Philippians 4:13

God overrode the learned helplessness of the Israelites and saved them from Egypt. Twelve spies were sent into the Promised Land. Imagine the dismay of the Israelites when 10 spies came back with a discouraging report: "We can't attack those people; they are stronger than we are" (Numbers 13:31). Now what? Their present circumstances were bleak, their prospects seemed hopeless, and they felt helpless because they were unable to do anything about it—or so they thought.

However, two of the spies didn't see it that way. Joshua and Caleb saw the land as exceedingly good (see 14:7). They could see with the eyes of faith that their enemies' protection was gone and that the Lord was with His people (see verse 9). God would win their battles for them. For their part, the Israelites had to overcome their fears by trusting God and obeying His Word.

Many people are defeated because of childhood messages they received from the world or from careless parents. *You can't do that; you better let me do it. You're not big enough. You'll never amount to anything.* It has been estimated that 95 percent of the world's population is pessimistic by nature. News anchors report the bad news and seldom share the good news. Three news helicopters and 15 police cars will follow a fugitive in a car pursuit for hours, but nobody is following the good guys and gals who set about their day encouraging others. Meteorologists predict a 35 percent chance for rain but seldom say there is a 65 percent chance for sunshine.

The world is obliterated with blessing snatchers. "Oh, I see you bought a new car. I bought one like that. It was a lemon." "So, you became a new Christian. Well, now you have an enemy you never had before!" There are also naysayers who claim it can't be done. Motivational speakers try to shed some light with clever little jingles: "If you think you are beaten, you are. If you think you dare not, you don't. If you like to win, but think you can't, it is almost certain you won't. If you think you'll lose, you're lost, for out in the world we find that success begins with a fellow's will. It's all in the state of mind. . . . Life's battles don't always go to the stronger or faster man. But sooner or later the man who wins is the man who thinks he can."[1]

Henry Ford once said, "Whether you think you can, or you think you can't—you're right." There is some truth to that axiom, but you don't overcome helplessness by the power of positive thinking, as beneficial as that may be for the natural man. You would still be limited by your own natural abilities. Christians aren't motivated by hype. They are motivated by Pentecostal vision that believes with God all things are possible, because if God wants it done, it can be done. "For nothing is impossible with God" (Luke 1:37 NLT), even the pregnancy of a virgin. You overcome helplessness by the power of God and by believing the truth. Someone once said that success comes in "cans" and failure comes in "cannots." On pages 128–129 are Twenty "Cans" of Success that will help you overcome your sense of helplessness.

Did the 10 spies walk by faith or by sight? What is the difference?

What kind of vision did Joshua and Caleb have in that same situation?

Why are there so many blessing-snatchers and naysayers?

For you, how is God an ever-present help in time of need?

What situations in your life right now do you need to see through the eyes of faith rather than through eyes of fear and helplessness?

Since this might seem like a great boast, see how quickly he adds: "I can do all things in Christ who strengthens me" [Philippians 4:13]. Any achievement I have had belongs not to me, but to the One who gave me strength.

John Chrysostom (AD 347–407)

Twenty "Cans" of Success

1. Why should I say I can't when the Bible says I can do all things through Christ who gives me strength (see Philippians 4:13)?

2. Why should I worry about my needs when I know that God will take care of all my needs according to His riches in glory in Christ Jesus (see Philippians 4:19)?

3. Why should I fear when the Bible says God has not given me a spirit of fear, but of power, love, and a sound mind (see 2 Timothy 1:7)?

4. Why should I lack faith to live for Christ when God has given me a measure of faith (see Romans 12:3)?

5. Why should I be weak when the Bible says that the Lord is the strength of my life and that I will display strength and take action because I know God (see Psalm 27:1; Daniel 11:32)?

6. Why should I allow Satan control over my life when He that is in me is greater than he that is in the world (see 1 John 4:4)?

7. Why should I accept defeat when the Bible says that God always leads me in victory (see 2 Corinthians 2:14)?

8. Why should I lack wisdom when I know that Christ became wisdom to me from God and God gives wisdom to me generously when I ask Him for it (see 1 Corinthians 1:30; James 1:5)?

9. Why should I be depressed when I can recall God's lovingkindness, compassion, and faithfulness, and have hope (see Lamentations 3:21, 23)?

10. Why should I worry and be upset when I can cast all my anxieties on Christ who cares for me (see 1 Peter 5:7)?

11. Why should I ever be in bondage knowing that Christ has set me free and where the Spirit of the Lord is, there is freedom (see Galatians 5:1; 2 Corinthians 3:17)?

12. Why should I feel condemned when the Bible says there is no condemnation for those who are in Christ Jesus (see Romans 8:1)?

13. Why should I feel alone when Jesus said He is with me always and He will never leave me nor forsake me (see Matthew 28:20; Hebrews 13:5)?

14. Why should I feel like I am cursed when the Bible says that Christ rescued me from the curse of the law that I might receive His Spirit by faith (see Galatians 3:13–14)?

15. Why should I be discontented when I, like Paul, can learn to be content whatever the circumstances (see Philippians 4:11)?

16. Why should I feel worthless when Christ became sin for me so that I might become the righteousness of God (see 2 Corinthians 5:21)?

17. Why should I feel helpless in the presence of others when I know that if God is for me, nobody or nothing greater can be against me (see Romans 8:31)?

18. Why should I be confused when God is the author of peace and He gives me knowledge through His Spirit who lives in me (see 1 Corinthians 2:12; 14:33)?

19. Why should I feel like a failure when I am more than a conqueror through Christ who loves me (see Romans 8:37)?

20. Why should I let the pressures of life bother me when I can take courage knowing that Jesus has overcome the world and its problems (see John 16:33)?

Overcoming Losses

The thought of suicide came to me as naturally then as the thought of improving life had come to me before. This thought was such a temptation that I had to use cunning against myself in order not to go through with it too hastily. I did not want to be in a hurry only because I wanted to use all my strength to untangle my thoughts. If I could not get them untangled, I told myself, I could always go through with it. And that I was, a fortunate man, carrying a rope from room to room, where I was alone every night as I undressed, so that I would not hang myself from the beam between the closets. And I quit going hunting with a gun, so that I would not be too easily tempted to rid myself of life. I myself did not know what I wanted. I was afraid of life. I struggled to get rid of it, and I hoped for something from it.

And this was happening to me at a time when, from all indications, I should have been considered a completely happy man; this was when I was not yet fifty years old. I had a good, loving, and beloved wife, fine children, and a large estate that was growing and expanding without any effort on my part. More than ever before I was respected by friends and acquaintances, praised by strangers, and I could claim a certain renown without really deluding myself.

—Leo Tolstoy in *Confessions*[1]

Dearest, I feel certain I am going mad again. I feel we can't go through another of those terrible times. And I shan't recover this time. I begin to hear voices, and I can't concentrate. So I am doing what seems the best thing to do. You have given me the greatest possible happiness. You have been in every way all that anyone could be. I don't think two people could have been happier till this terrible disease came. I can't fight any longer.

—The final letter from author Virginia Woolf to her husband[2]

My wife was freed from five years of clinical depression after working through the Steps to Freedom in Christ. The two years before this, my wife had been institutionalized for a week and had been drugged to the extent that she was a zombie. She was taking more than nine medications for her illness, more than 30 pills daily. Just two weeks prior to meeting with our pastor to work through the seven steps, I gave up and decided to quit my marriage of more than 20 years. My son shamed me into staying, and I thank God every day for having him do so. After working through the seven steps and praying for a renewing of my wife's mind, we saw a healing by God. My wife was able to stop all of the medications except for two. She is now able to live her life fully. Whereas before she hid in our room and wished her life was over.

—Email sent to the author

I am 27 years old, on my second marriage and have five kids. I have been dealing with depression for most of my life. I have tried many things to stop the pain and overdosed on meds several times. My church was doing the *Victory Over the Darkness* video series, and when I saw the lesson "the Battle for Our Minds," I realized that I wasn't crazy. I have always heard voices in my head but was afraid to tell anyone. My pastor led me through the Steps to Freedom in Christ. The voices are gone, and I am a new person. I wake up with a song of praise every morning.

—Email sent to author

Daily Readings

1. Reacting to Losses	Mark 10:32–34
2. Surviving the Crisis	Job 3:1–26
3. Identifying Losses	Acts 9:1–31
4. The Elijah Complex	1 Kings 19:1–18
5. Commitment to Overcome Depression	John 5:1–18

1

Reacting to Losses

Mark 10:32–34

Key Point

No crisis can destroy us, but they do reveal who we are.

Key Verse

For our light and momentary troubles are achieving for us an eternal glory that far outweighs them all.

2 Corinthians 4:17

Nobody likes the idea of impermanence. We live every day with the assumption that tomorrow will be the same. We make plans for the future with the thought that we will have our health and the same job, family, and friends. James says otherwise. "Now listen, you who say, 'Today or tomorrow we will go to this or that city, spend a year there, carry on business and make money.' Why, you do not even know what will happen tomorrow. What is your life? You are a mist that appears for a little while and then vanishes. Instead, you ought to say, 'If it is the Lord's will, we will live and do this or that'" (James 4:13–15).

Only God is permanent—everything else is changing. We are time-oriented people by nature who are in the process of learning to see life from God's eternal perspective. On three occasions Jesus told His disciples that He was going to Jerusalem, where He would be betrayed and crucified. The first time the disciples essentially denied Jesus, and Peter even rebuked Him (see Mark 8:31–32). The second time they didn't understand and were afraid to talk about it (see Mark 9:32).

On the third occasion, the disciples were terrified. Their life as they knew it was soon to be over (see Mark 10:32). We all go through a similar reaction when a crisis abruptly ends an established lifestyle. Usually, the crisis is defined by a significant loss that can be real, threatened, or imagined.

Crisis Reaction Cycle

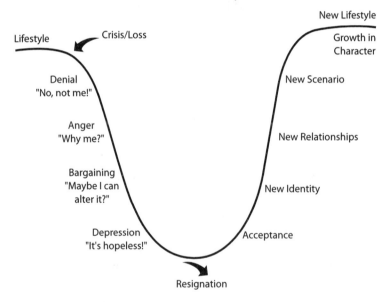

Our first response is denial, which can last for 3 seconds or 30 years. Our initial reaction is a sense of disbelief—*No, not me!* Then we get angry and wonder, *How can this happen to me?* The anger often turns to bargaining as we think, *Maybe I can alter what happened.* Finally, we feel depressed when we are unable to reverse the consequences of the loss. Reaction to losses is the primary cause for depression. No crisis can destroy us, but it will reveal who we are.

Learning to overcome losses is a critical part of our spiritual growth. Everything we now have in this temporal world we shall someday lose. The critical questions are whether we are going to choose the path of resignation and allow the loss to negatively affect us for the rest of our lives, or whether we are going to accept what we cannot change and grow through the crisis. A wise person once said, "A bend in the road is not the end of the road unless you fail to make the turn."

What were the disciples' reactions when Jesus told them that He was going to be betrayed and crucified (see Mark 8:31–32; 9:32; 10:32)?

How can the loss of health, a spouse, a date, a job, a leg, and so forth lead to depression?

How can accepting what we cannot change lead to growth in character and a better lifestyle than before the loss?

What changes have you had to adapt to recently? In what ways have those changes been unsettling?

_____

_____

_____

How should you move on after a significant loss in your life?

_____

_____

_____

James is not trying to take away our freedom to decide, but he is showing us that it is not just what we want that matters. We need God's grace to complement our efforts and ought to rely not on them but on God's love for us. As it says in Proverbs: "Do not boast about tomorrow, for you do not know what a day may bring forth."

John Chrysostom (AD 347–407)

2

Surviving the Crisis

Job 3:1–26

Key Point
"He is no fool who gives what he cannot keep to gain that which he cannot lose" (Jim Elliot).

Key Verse
I consider everything a loss because of the surpassing worth of knowing Christ Jesus my Lord.

Philippians 3:8

Job suffered the loss of everything except his life. He was in the pit of depression and wished he had never been born. He did not accept his present condition; instead, he resigned and gave up on life (see Job 3). We all experience losses in our lives. We need to learn how to accept what we cannot change and grow through the crisis. How well we handle a loss is determined by how we process three mental constructs.

The first mental construct is *permanence*. The speed of our recovery is greatly affected by whether we think the consequences of the crisis will have a short-term or long-term negative effect on us. The loss is permanent, but it doesn't have to affect us permanently. There is the potential to grow through every crisis.

Suppose your new employer is irritable. If you think it is just a passing mood, it is a short-term problem and will have little impact on you. However, if you think your boss is always irritable, it is a long-term problem. You can respond to this crisis in several ways. You can decide to ignore him, which is denial. You can decide to be irritable back, which is responding in anger. You can try to appease him, which is bargaining. You can decide you are stuck with this irritable person whom you cannot change, which is depressing. You decide to quit, which is resignation. Or, you can decide to love him and learn to live with him, which is acceptance.

The second mental construct is *pervasiveness*. You will recover slowly if you think your whole life has been ruined as a result of the crisis. If you experience one loss, you are not a loser. If you fail to accomplish one goal, you are not a failure. If you get laid off at work, you are not unemployable. It is natural to grieve for what you have lost, and grieving is an important part of the recovery process. However, a prolonged depression due to losses signifies an undue and unhealthy attachment to people, places, and things that you have no right or ability to control.

The third mental construct is *personalization*. Blaming yourself for every loss will keep you in a rut. If you experience loss in one area, don't generalize it and create a total crisis. Keep your loss specific. If you experience a crisis today, don't allow it to affect you tomorrow. Keep short accounts. If the world is disintegrating around you, don't accept the blame when it's not appropriate. If you are suffering the consequences of a bad decision, then change what you can, minimize your losses, and move on.

Traumatic losses often cause us to reevaluate who we are, especially if our identity has been tied up with what we have lost—such as when we lose a job or a spouse. A crisis can deepen our walk with God and solidify our identity in Christ. Losses also precipitate the need for new relationships and a change of scenery. These changes are probably necessary for our growth in Christ, but we may not make them unless we are forced to do so.

Read Job 1:13–19. Using Job as an example for a significant loss, how can you reprocess your loss by rethinking those three mental constructs starting with *permanence*?

How can you reprocess your loss by rethinking through *pervasiveness*?

How can you reprocess your loss by rethinking through *personalization*? (Note that Job's three friends tried to convince him that his suffering and depression was due to his sin!)

As a believer, what can you never lose? How can that truth help you recover from any temporal loss?

Loses will have an impact on believers just like unbelievers. So how can you prepare yourself for future losses so the impact is not so devastating?

_____

_____

_____

In yielding to evils that are brief and passing, they do not destroy the good which is great and eternal, for "the suffering of the present time are not worthy to be compared," the apostle says, "with the glory to come that will be revealed in us" [2 Corinthians 4:17]. And he also says: "Our present light affliction, which is for the moment, prepares for us an eternal weight of glory that is beyond measure."

Augustine of Hippo (AD 354–430)

3

Identifying Losses

Acts 9:1–31

Key Point

Whether losses are real, threatened, or imagined, the emotional effect is the same.

Key Verse

"Who are you, Lord?"

Acts 9:5

After Paul was struck down by God, he went away for three years. It must have been a time of deep remorse for persecuting the Church, but it was also a time to grieve. He had lost everything he had worked for. His reputation in the Jewish community was gone, and so were all his friends and associates. Eventually, he would consider those losses to be nothing in comparison to what he gained in Christ Jesus.

Most losses are easy to recognize, but some aren't. Changing jobs or moving to a new location can precipitate depression. Even though both changes could improve your social standing and financial base, there are losses in the transition. You probably had meaningful attachments to family, church, friends, and familiar places, which you no longer have. Many losses are multifaceted. For instance, the loss of a job could also include the loss of wages, social status, respect, friendships, and colleagues.

In order to move beyond denial and continue the grieving process, you have to identify the losses. Start by separating real losses from those that are threatened or imagined. In a real loss you can face the truth, grieve the loss, and make the necessary changes that make it possible to go on living in a meaningful way. You cannot process an imagined loss in the same way, because there is no basis in reality. Imagined losses are based on suspicions or lies that you believe or presumptions that you make up. If you imagine that something negative will happen and live accordingly, it will have the same effect on you emotionally as though it actually happened. False prophecies and lies are the basis for many depressed people.

Threatened losses have the potential of being real losses, such as the possibility of a layoff at work or a spouse threatening to leave. Such threats can precipitate depressed states of the mind when believed. It is helpful to convert threatened losses to real losses in your mind and ask yourself a question: *Can I live with that?* This prepares you to accept the idea of impermanence. The answer to that question should be, *Yes I can!* Of course you can, because "God will meet all your needs" (Philippians 4:19), and you "can do all things through Christ" who gives you strength (4:13 NKJV). People all over the world are facing similar crises that are real and have survived. These are growth issues, not terminal issues, if you understand life from an eternal perspective.

The natural process to any crisis is to deny that it is happening, get angry when it does, and then try to alter the situation by bargaining with God and others. The goal is not to try to undo it all; the goal is to make the best of what you have. What you cannot do is bypass the grieving process, but you can shorten it by allowing yourself to feel the full force of the loss. The fact that many losses are depressing and painful is reality. It hurts to lose something of value. To say you are doing fine, or that what you lost had no value, is to deny reality. Funerals honor the memory of loved ones, but they also facilitate the grieving process in a safe environment.

What did Paul lose when he was struck down? How hard do you think it was for Paul to realize that his zeal for God was totally misplaced—leading him to conclude that he was the chief of all sinners?

What are some of the hidden losses when you graduate from high school? Move out of the state? Get dumped by a friend? Lose a limb in an accident?

What happens if we don't allow ourselves to feel the full brunt of losses?

What imagined or threatened losses have you had to deal with? How did you, or are you, processing that loss?

A prolonged depression can signify an overattachment to people, places, and things that you have no right or ability to control. How can you value those things without becoming overly attached?

The afflictions come not only from enemies but even from our own households and friends. These things are permitted by God, not for our defeat but for our discipline.

John Chrysostom (AD 347–407)

4

The Elijah Complex

1 Kings 19:1–18

Key Point

Believing the enemy's lies after a mountaintop experience will lead you to a place God has not called you.

Key Verse

Elijah was afraid and ran for his life.

1 Kings 19:3

Elijah was truly a man of God. He had just witnessed God display His power against the prophets of Baal (see 1 Kings 18:16–45). When Jezebel heard of it, she sent a messenger to Elijah who said, "May the gods deal with me, be it ever so severely, if by this time tomorrow I do not make your life like that of one of them" (19:2). This incredible man of God was afraid and ran for his life. He left his servant in Beersheba and went a day's journey into the desert. Then he cried out in despair, "I have had enough, LORD . . . take my life; I am no better than my ancestors" (verse 4). Then he lay down and went to sleep.

Elijah was exhibiting many of the classic signs of depression. He was afraid, fatigued, felt like a helpless failure, and was isolated and all alone. That can easily happen after a mountaintop experience. Brimming with confidence and flushed with victory, Elijah suddenly found himself vulnerable. Confidence in God can easily turn to self-confidence when we let our guard down. God in His mercy prescribed some food and rest for His discouraged warrior. "All at once an angel touched him and said, 'Get up and eat.' He looked around, and there by his head was a cake of bread baked over hot coals, and a jar of water" (verses 5–6).

We can become depressed when our electrolytes are depleted and our bodies are malfunctioning for lack of nutrition, as was probably the case for Elijah. God addressed these deficiencies by prescribing food and rest. Our mental health is dependent on a proper balance of rest, exercise, and diet. In addition, Elijah was probably suffering from post-adrenal exhaustion. Our adrenal glands respond to stress by secreting cortisone into our bloodstream. If the stress becomes too great, our adrenal glands can't keep up. Stress becomes distress, and our system breaks down. This often happens to driven people who work until they collapse in exhaustion and depression.

However, the precipitating cause of Elijah's depression was not physical. This faithful servant had always been obedient to God. Now the Lord asked him twice, "What are you doing here, Elijah?" (verses 9, 13). Elijah replied, "I have been very zealous for the Lord God Almighty. The Israelites have rejected your covenant, torn down your altars, and put your prophets to death with the sword. I am the only one left, and now they are trying to kill me too" (verse 10). Elijah ran because he believed a lie, not because God sent him into the wilderness. Further, Elijah wasn't the only one left—there were 7,000 others who had not bowed their knees to Baal (see verse 18).

God was not asking Elijah (or us) to establish His kingdom program or bring judgment on those who had not kept His covenant. He was asking Elijah (and us) to trust Him and follow where He led. He will bring judgment and establish His kingdom in His way and in His timing—it is neither for us to decide nor accomplish. Although Elijah was zealous for

God's work, he was wrong to assume sole responsibility for getting the job done. Those who buy into the Elijah complex are vulnerable to the enemy's lies and may end up mentally depressed and physically exhausted.

Review the story of Elijah in 1 Kings 19:1–18. What led to Elijah's fleeing in fear and his subsequent state of despair?

_____

_____

_____

What was wrong with Elijah's thinking?

_____

_____

_____

What is post-adrenal exhaustion and what are the treatments?

_____

_____

_____

Jezebel's curse was a lie and curses can have no effect on us unless we believe them. What curses/lies have led you to run like Elijah?

_____

_____

_____

_____

How have you bought into the Elijah complex and attempted to take on God's responsibility?

_____

_____

_____

For God delivers us from afflictions not when we are no longer afflicted . . . (Paul says "we are afflicted in every way," as though there were never a time when we were not afflicted), but when in our affliction we are not crushed because of God's help. "To be afflicted," according to a colloquial usage of the Hebrews, has the meaning of a critical circumstance that happens to us without our free choice, while "to be crushed" implies our free choice and that it has been conquered by affliction and given into its power. And so Paul is right when he says, "We are afflicted in every way but not crushed."

Origen (AD 184–253)

5

Commitment to Overcome Depression

John 5:1–18

Key Point

The key to any cure is commitment.

Key Verse

I say these things while I am still in the world, so that they may have the full measure of my joy within them.

John 17:13

A psychosomatic illness is one caused by a mental state, and more people are sick for that reason than any other. At the heart of psychosomatic illness is the soul, and that can be restored. "Therefore we do not lose heart. Though outwardly we are wasting away, yet inwardly we are being renewed day by day" (2 Corinthians 4:16). In other words, there is hope if you turn to God and assume your responsibility. How do you do this?

First, *commit yourself to complete recovery.* The key to any cure is commitment. Decide to believe that you can do all things through Christ who strengthens you (see Philippians 4:13), and then do it. You can't look for somebody else to cure you, or blame someone else for your lack of follow-through.

Second, *commit yourself to pray first about everything.* The old nature will seek every possible natural explanation and cure first. Jesus told us to seek first His kingdom and His righteousness and "all these things will be given to you as well" (Matthew 6:33). The first thing believers should do about anything is pray.

Third, *commit yourself to having an intimate relationship with your heavenly Father.* This requires repentance and faith in God. You can resolve your personal and spiritual conflicts by going through the Steps to Freedom in Christ. To be mentally healthy, you must have a true understanding of who God is and be rightly related to Him.

Fourth, *commit yourself as a child of God.* Don't think that doctors and hospitals take care of the body and the Church takes care of the soul. You need a wholistic answer or psychosomatic illnesses will never get treated. The second basic standard for mental health is to have a biblical understanding of who you are in Christ and to know what it means to be a child of God. You cannot consistently feel or behave in a way that is inconsistent with what you believe about yourself.

Fifth, *commit your body to God.* If the previous four steps do not cure your psychosomatic illness, then consult a medical doctor for a complete physical examination. There are many forms of biological depression that can be diagnosed and treated. Disorders of the endocrine system can produce symptoms of depression. These include the possibility of low blood sugar, malfunctioning pituitary gland, adrenal exhaustion, and problems related to the female reproductive system. Work toward a proper balance of nutrition, exercise, and diet. At this stage, medication may be necessary to cure the body.

Sixth, *commit yourself to the renewing of your mind.* Mental depression stems from a negative view of yourself, your circumstances, and the future. These false perceptions can only be overcome as you are transformed by the renewing of your mind (see Romans 12:2) and by choosing to believe the truth (see Philippians 4:6–9).

Seventh, *commit yourself to good behavior.* Make realistic plans to be involved with your family and church members. Live a responsible life by following through on your commitments. Schedule meaningful activities and exercise.

Finally, *commit yourself to overcome every loss, whether real, imagined, or threatened.* Be aware that abstract losses such as reputation, social standing, and friendships are harder to identify. You can choose to overcome every loss by deepening your walk with God, reaffirming who you really are in Christ, growing in character, and by developing a more Christian lifestyle.

Why are so many people ill today because of lifestyle and psychosomatic reasons?

_____

_____

_____

_____

Why is commitment so essential to overcome psychosomatic illnesses?

_____

_____

_____

Why is it critical for healing to have a proper understanding of who you are in Christ and have an intimate relationship with your heavenly Father?

_____

_____

_____

_____

What lifestyle changes do you need to make in order to live a healthy life?

_____

_____

_____

Are you willing to assume your responsibility for your health and to take whatever steps it takes to be mentally and emotionally healthy? Why or why not?

_____

_____

_____

_____

A man who has his own interest at heart will therefore be especially concerned for his soul and will spare no pains to keep it stainless and true to itself. If his body is wasted by hunger or by its struggles with heat and cold, if it is afflicted by illness or suffers violence from anyone, he will pay little attention to it, and echoing the words of Paul, he will say in each of his adversities: "But though our outward man is corrupted, yet the inward man is renewed day by day." . . . But, if a man would also have mercy upon his body as being a possession necessary to the soul and its cooperator in carrying on the life on earth, he will occupy himself with its needs only so far as is required to preserve it and keep it vigorous by moderate care in the service of the soul.

Basil the Great (AD 330–379)

154

Do You Want to Get Well?

There are three types of people who cannot be helped. The first are those who will not acknowledge they have a problem or realize their need for God. The second are those who know they are in trouble, but their pride won't let them ask for the help they need. Their self-sufficiency is keeping them from finding their sufficiency in Christ. God has a way of bringing such people to the end of their resources, like the overly confident Paul who had to be struck down before he found his sufficiency in Christ (see 2 Corinthians 1:8–10).

The third type are those who really don't want to get well. Such was the case of the man who was an invalid for 38 years. He would lie by the pool of Bethesda, where the blind, the lame, and the paralyzed came to be healed. Supposedly, an angel would come and stir the waters, and whoever was in it at the time was healed. The Lord asked him, "Do you want to get well?" (John 5:6). That was a profound question, not a cruel one. The invalid answered with an excuse. There was no one to put him in the water, or someone always got in ahead of him! This man showed no faith in God, but the Lord in His sovereignty chose to heal him anyway. Jesus warned him to stop sinning, for the eternal consequences of sin were far worse than his physical ailment. To show his gratitude, the man turned Him in for healing him on the Sabbath!

Jesus took away the man's excuse and probably his source of income through begging. Such people have a built-in excuse for not rising above the circumstances. Their illness solicits attention and pity from others. If the invalid really wanted to get well, he would have found a way to get into that pool. Those who want to get well should make whatever commitment it takes to overcome their infirmities. If we have to swallow our pride and humble ourselves, we do it. If we have to submit to a process that trusted people advise us to take, we do it. If we have to give up an unrighteous lifestyle, we do it. If we have to ask others to forgive us, we do it. If we need to forgive others, we do it. If we need to persevere under pressure, we do it.

We do whatever it takes to become the person God created us to be, because Jesus did what it took for us to be alive and free in Him. The test of our character is determined by what it takes to stop us from pursuing our convictions. "We count as blessed those who have persevered" (James 5:11).

Leader's Tips

The following are some guidelines for leaders to follow when using the VICTORY SERIES studies with a small group. Generally, the ideal size for a group is between 10 and 20 people, which is small enough for meaningful fellowship but large enough for dynamic group interaction. It is typically best to stop opening up the group to members after the second session and invite them to join the next study after the six weeks are complete.

Structuring Your Time Together

For best results, ensure that all participants have a copy of the book. They should be encouraged to read the material and consider the questions and applications on their own before the group session. If participants have to miss a meeting, they should keep abreast of the study on their own. The group session reinforces what they learned and offers the valuable perspectives of others. Learning best takes place in the context of committed relationships, so do more than just share answers. Take the time to care and share with one another. You might want to use the first week to distribute material and give everyone a chance to tell others who they are.

If you discussed just one topic a week, it would take several years to finish the VICTORY SERIES. If you did five a week, it is possible to complete the whole series in 48 weeks. All the books in the series were written with a six-week study in mind. However, each group is different and each will have to discover its own pace. If too many participants come unprepared, you may have to read, or at least summarize, the text before discussing the questions and applications.

It would be great if this series was used for a church staff or Bible study at work and could be done one topic at a time, five days a week. However, most study groups will likely be meeting weekly. It is best to start with a time of sharing and prayer for one another. Start with the text or Bible passage for each topic and move to the discussion questions and application. Take time at the end to summarize what has been covered, and dismiss in prayer.

Group Dynamics

Getting a group of people actively involved in discussing critical issues of the Christian life is very rewarding. Not only does group interaction help to create interest, stimulate thinking, and encourage effective learning, but it is also vital for building quality relationships within the group. Only as people begin to share their thoughts and feelings will they begin to build bonds of friendship and support.

It is important to set some guidelines at the beginning of the study, as follows:

- There are no wrong questions.
- Everyone should feel free to share his or her ideas without recrimination.
- Focus on the issues and not on personalities.
- Try not to dominate the discussions or let others do so.
- Personal issues shared in the group must remain in the group.
- Avoid gossiping about others in or outside the group.
- Side issues should be diverted to the end of the class for those who wish to linger and discuss them further.
- Above all, help each other grow in Christ.

Some may find it difficult to share with others, and that is okay. It takes time to develop trust in any group. A leader can create a more open and sharing atmosphere by being appropriately vulnerable himself or herself. A good leader doesn't have all the answers and doesn't need to for this study. Some questions raised are extremely difficult to answer and have been puzzled over for years by educated believers. We will never have all the answers to every question in this age, but that does not preclude discussion over eternal matters. Hopefully, it will cause some to dig deeper.

Leading the Group

The following tips can be helpful in making group interaction a positive learning opportunity for everyone:

- When a question or comment is raised that is off the subject, suggest that you will bring it up again at the end of the class if anyone is still interested.

- When someone talks too much, direct a few questions specifically to other people, making sure not to put any shy people on the spot. Talk privately with the "dominator" and ask for cooperation in helping to draw out the quieter group members.

- Hopefully the participants have already written their answers to the discussion questions and will share that when asked. If most haven't come prepared, give them some time to personally reflect on what has been written and the questions asked.

- If someone asks a question that you don't know how to answer, admit it and move on. If the question calls for insight about personal experience, invite group members to comment. If the question requires specialized knowledge, offer to look for an answer before the next session. (Make sure to follow up the next session.)

- When group members disagree with you or each other, remind them that it is possible to disagree without becoming disagreeable. To help clarify the issues while maintaining a climate of mutual acceptance, encourage those on opposite sides to restate what they have heard the other person(s) saying about the issue. Then invite each side to evaluate how accurately they feel their position was presented. Ask group members to identify as many points as possible related to the topic on which both sides agree, and then lead the group in examining other Scriptures related to the topic, looking for common ground that they can all accept.

- Finally, urge group members to keep an open heart and mind and a willingness to continue loving one another while learning more about the topic at hand.

If the disagreement involves an issue on which your church has stated a position, be sure that stance is clearly and positively presented. This should be done not to squelch dissent but to ensure that there is no confusion over where your church stands.

Notes

Session Two

1. Dr. and Mrs. Howard Taylor, *Hudson Taylor's Spiritual Secret* (Chicago: Moody Press, 1990), pp. 158–164.

Session Five

1. William Styron, *The Darkness Visible* (New York: Random House, 1990).

Chapter 2 The Basis for Our Hope

1. Lewis Mumford (1895–1990), *The Conduct of Life* (New York: Harcourt, Brace and Company, 1951).

Chapter 5 Overcoming Helplessness

1. Walter D. Wintle, "Thinking," first published in 1905 by Unity Tract Society, Unity School of Christianity.

Session Six

1. Leo Tolstoy, *Confessions* (New York: W.W. Norton, 1983), pp. 28–29.
2. Anne Olivier Bell and Andrew McNeillie, eds., *The Diary of Virginia Woolf* (New York: Harcourt, Brace, Jovanovich, 1984), p. 226.

Victory Series Scope
and Sequence Overview

The Victory Series is composed of eight studies that create a comprehensive discipleship course. Each study builds on the previous one and provides six sessions of material. These can be used by an individual or in a small group setting. There are leader's tips at the back of each study for those leading a small group.

The following scope and sequence overview gives a brief summary of the content of each of the eight studies in the Victory Series. Some studies also include articles related to the content of that study.

The Victory Series

Study 1   God's Story for You: Discover the Person God Created You to Be

---

Session One: The Story of Creation
Session Two: The Story of the Fall
Session Three: The Story of Salvation
Session Four: The Story of God's Sanctification
Session Five: The Story of God's Transforming Power
Session Six: The Story of God

Study 2   Your New Identity: A Transforming Union With God

Session One: A New Life "in Christ"
Session Two: A New Understanding of God's Character
Session Three: A New Understanding of God's Nature
Session Four: A New Relationship With God
Session Five: A New Humanity
Session Six: A New Beginning

Study 3   Your Foundation in Christ: Live by the Power of the Spirit

---

Session One: Liberating Truth
Session Two: The Nature of Faith
Session Three: Living Boldly
Session Four: Godly Relationships
Session Five: Freedom of Forgiveness
Session Six: Living by the Spirit

Study 4   Renewing Your Mind: Become More Like Christ

Session One: Being Transformed
Session Two: Living Under Grace
Session Three: Overcoming Anger
Session Four: Overcoming Anxiety
Session Five: Overcoming Depression
Session Six: Overcoming Losses

Coming Soon

Study 5   Growing in Christ: Deepen Your Relationship With Jesus

---

Session One: Spiritual Discernment
Session Two: Spiritual Gifts
Session Three: Growing Through Committed Relationships
Session Four: Overcoming Sexual Bondage
Session Five: Overcoming Chemical Addiction
Session Six: Suffering for Righteousness' Sake

Study 6   Your Life in Christ: Walk in Freedom by Faith

Session One: God's Will
Session Two: Faith Appraisal (Part 1)
Session Three: Faith Appraisal (Part 2)
Session Four: Spiritual Leadership
Session Five: Discipleship Counseling
Session Six: The Kingdom of God

Study 7 Your Authority in Christ: Overcoming the Enemy

Session One: The Origin of Evil
Session Two: God and Evil Spirits
Session Three: Overcoming the Opposition
Session Four: Kingdom Sovereignty
Session Five: The Armor of God (Part 1)
Session Six: The Armor of God (Part 2)

Study 8   Your Ultimate Victory: Standing Strong in the Faith

Session One: The Battle for Our Minds
Session Two: The Lure of Knowledge and Power
Session Three: Overcoming Temptation
Session Four: Overcoming Accusation
Session Five: Overcoming Deception
Session Six: Degrees of Spiritual Vulnerability

Books and Resources

Dr. Neil T. Anderson

Core Material

Victory Over the Darkness with study guide, audiobook, and DVD. With over 1,300,000 copies in print, this core book explains who you are in Christ, how to walk by faith in the power of the Holy Spirit, how to be transformed by the renewing of your mind, how to experience emotional freedom, and how to relate to one another in Christ.

The Bondage Breaker with study guide, audiobook, and DVD. With over 1,300,000 copies in print, this book explains spiritual warfare, what our protection is, ways that we are vulnerable, and how we can live a liberated life in Christ.

Breaking Through to Spiritual Maturity. This curriculum teaches the basic message of Freedom in Christ Ministries.

Discipleship Counseling with DVD. This book combines the concepts of discipleship and counseling and teaches the practical integration of theology and psychology for helping Christians resolve their personal and spiritual conflicts through repentance and faith in God.

Steps to Freedom in Christ and interactive video. This discipleship counseling tool helps Christians resolve their personal and spiritual conflicts through genuine repentance and faith in God.

Restored. This book is an expansion of the *Steps to Freedom in Christ*, and offers more explanation and illustrations.

Walking in Freedom. This book is a 21-day devotional that we use for follow-up after leading someone through the Steps to Freedom.

Freedom in Christ is a discipleship course for Sunday school classes and small groups. The course comes with a teacher's guide, a student guide, and a DVD covering 12 lessons and the Steps to Freedom in Christ. This course is designed to enable new and stagnant believers to resolve personal and spiritual conflicts and be established alive and free in Christ.

The Bondage Breaker DVD Experience is also a discipleship course for Sunday School classes and small groups. It is similar to the one above, but the lessons are 15 minutes instead of 30 minutes.

The Daily Discipler. This practical systematic theology is a culmination of all of Dr. Anderson's books covering the major doctrines of the Christian faith and the problems Christians face. It is a five-day-per-week, one-year study that will thoroughly ground believers in their faith.

Specialized Books

The Bondage Breaker, the Next Step. This book has several testimonies of people finding their freedom from all kinds of problems, with commentary by Dr. Anderson. It is an important learning tool for encouragers.

Overcoming Addictive Behavior, with Mike Quarles. This book explores the path to addiction and how a Christian can overcome addictive behaviors.

Overcoming Depression, with Joanne Anderson. This book explores the nature of depression, which is a body, soul, and spirit problem and presents a wholistic answer for overcoming this "common cold" of mental illness.

Liberating Prayer. This book helps believers understand the confusion in their minds when it comes time to pray, and why listening in prayer may be more important than talking.

Daily in Christ, with Joanne Anderson. This popular daily devotional is also being used by thousands of Internet subscribers every day.

Who I Am in Christ. In 36 short chapters, this book describes who you are in Christ and how He meets your deepest needs.

Freedom from Addiction, with Mike and Julia Quarles. Using Mike's testimony, this book explains the nature of chemical addictions and how to overcome them in Christ.

One Day at a Time, with Mike and Julia Quarles. This devotional helps those who struggle with addictive behaviors and explains how to discover the grace of God on a daily basis.

Freedom from Fear, with Rich Miller. This book explains anxiety disorders and how to overcome them.

Setting Your Church Free, with Charles Mylander. This book offers guidelines and encouragement for resolving seemingly impossible corporate conflicts in the church and also provides leaders with a primary means for church growth—releasing the power of God in the church.

Setting Your Marriage Free, with Dr. Charles Mylander. This book explains God's divine plan for marriage and the steps that couples can take to resolve their difficulties.

Christ-Centered Therapy, with Dr. Terry and Julie Zuehlke. This is a textbook explaining the practical integration of theology and psychology for professional counselors.

Getting Anger Under Control, with Rich Miller. This book explains the basis for anger and how to control it.

Grace that Breaks the Chains, with Rich Miller and Paul Travis. This book explains legalism and how to overcome it.

Winning the Battle Within. This book shares God's standards for sexual conduct, the path to sexual addiction, and how to overcome sexual strongholds.

The Path to Reconciliation. God has given the church the ministry of reconciliation. This book explains what that is and how it can be accomplished.

Rough Road to Freedom. This is a book of Dr. Anderson's memoirs.

For more information, contact Freedom In Christ Ministries at the following:

Canada: freedominchrist@sasktel.net or www.ficm.ca

India: isactara@vsnl.com

Switzerland: info@freiheitinchristus.ch or www.freiheitinchristus.ch

United Kingdom: info@ficm.org.uk or www.ficm.org.uk

United States: info@ficm.org or www.ficm.org

International: www.ficminternational.org

Dr. Anderson: www.discipleshipcounsel.com

Index

Adam, 109
Ambrose, 100
Ambrosiaster, 68, 80
anxiety disorders, 109, 169
Augustine of Hippo, 44, 142

Baal, 147, 148
Basil the Great, 20, 24, 154
Bede, 76, 92, 120
Beersheba, 147

Cain, 109
Caleb, 125, 127
Cassiodorus, 112
Chrysostom, John, 56, 88, 128, 138, 146
Clement of Alexandria, 72
Confessions, 131, 161
cortisone, 148
Cyril of Alexandria, 48

David, 30, 50, 62, 110, 114, 115
defense mechanisms, 17, 18, 19, 20
denial, 59, 136, 140, 144
depression, 6, 9, 33, 61, 67, 107–29, 132, 133,
    136–37, 139, 140, 141, 143, 146, 148,
    151–55, 164, 168
Darkness Visible, The (book), 107, 161
Discipleship Counseling (book), 9, 32, 164,
    167
discipline(d), 8, 54, 146

discipline(s), spiritual, 9
double-minded, 6, 25, 84, 85, 87, 89–92, 94

Early Church, 56
Egypt, 122, 125
electrolytes, 148
Elijah, 6, 133, 147–50
Elliot, Jim, 139
endocrine system, 152
endurance, 54
entrophy, law of, 85
escape mechanisms, 97
Ezra, 12, 29–30

flesh patterns, 17, 18, 19, 20
flesh, the, 7, 14, 42, 52
Ford, Henry, 126
Freedom in Christ Discipleship Course,
    32–33, 167–68
fruit of the Spirit, 25, 66, 76, 78, 86

godly desires, 69–71
godly goals, 69–72

Hilary of Arles, 116, 124
hora, 42

imagined losses, 136, 143, 144, 153
indiscriminate expression, 62
inferiority complex, 18

171

Irenaeus, 28, 32, 96
Israel(ites), 30, 48, 50, 62, 78, 90, 98, 122, 123, 125–26, 148

James, 30, 89–90, 104, 135, 138
Jerusalem, 136
Jezebel, 147, 149
Job, 139, 141
Joshua, 89, 90–91, 125, 127
Judeo-Christian, 66
justified, 42

law, 5, 16, 20, 30, 31, 36, 41–44, 48, 96, 124, 129
Lincoln, Abraham, 78
Living Free in Christ (conference), 32
Luther, Martin, 78, 115

Melanchthon, Philipp, 78
merimna, 89, 90
merimnao, 89, 90
merizo, 90
metamorphosis, 14
moneychangers, 78
Mosaic Law, 42. *See also* law.
Moses, 122, 123
Mumford, Lewis, 113, 161

natural person/man, 94, 95, 126
New Age movement, 121
New Testament, 42, 43, 89
nous, 90

Old Testament, 42, 43, 44, 56
omnipresent, 114
omniscient, 114
Origen, 16, 40, 150

Paul, 11, 14, 17, 19, 21, 25, 26, 30, 39, 40, 50, 56, 62, 66, 71, 74, 80, 86, 101, 112, 129, 143, 145, 150, 154, 155
Pentecost, 50, 126
permanence, 139–40, 141
persecution, 53, 54, 120
personalization, 140, 141
pervasiveness, 140, 141
Peter, 73, 74, 101, 136
petition, 25–26, 101

Pharaoh, 122
Pharisees, 41, 43, 94, 96
Philistine, 62
post-adrenal, 148, 149
prayer, 25–26, 50, 101, 103, 104–5, 158, 168
Promised Land, 125
psychosomatic illnesses, 62, 89, 105, 151, 152, 153

real losses, 136, 143, 144, 153
renunciation, 56
requests, 26, 101
righteous indignation, 6, 60, 77–81
righteous(ness), 40, 42–43, 54, 76, 78, 80, 85, 86, 87, 99, 101, 102, 104, 105, 118, 119, 129, 152, 164

Sabbath, 155
Samuel, 61–62
Saul, 62, 63, 115
second law of thermodynamics, 85
self-talk, 114, 116
sheep, 49–51, 121
Shema, 30
shepherd, 49–51, 121, 124
smartphone, 11
spiritual gifts, 73, 74, 164
Steps to Freedom in Christ, the, 9, 27, 32, 102, 103, 132, 152, 167, 168
strongholds, 5, 9, 12, 17–19, 169
Styron, William, 107, 161
suppress(ing), 61–63, 96

Temple, the, 44, 78
thanksgiving, 26, 101
threatened losses, 136, 143, 144, 145, 153
Tolstoy, Leo, 131, 161
torah, 42
transformation, 11, 13, 14, 15, 57
Twenty "Cans" of Success, 126, 128–29

Victorinus, Gaius Marius, 52, 64

Woolf, Virginia, 132, 161

yoke(d), 41, 46–48
Young, Edith Lillian, 59

Notes

Notes

Dr. Neil T. Anderson was formerly the chairman of the Practical Theology Department at Talbot School of Theology. In 1989, he founded Freedom in Christ Ministries, which now has staff and offices in various countries around the world. He is currently on the Freedom in Christ Ministries International Board, which oversees this global ministry. For more information about Dr. Anderson and his ministry, visit his website at www.ficminternational.org.

Also From
Neil T. Anderson

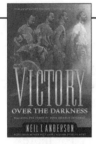

This bestselling landmark book gives you practical, productive ways to discover who you are in Christ. When you realize the power of your true identity, you can shed the burdens of your past, stand against evil influences, and become the person Christ empowers you to be.

Victory Over the Darkness

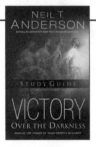

Great for small group or individual use, these thought-provoking personal reflection questions and applications for each chapter of *Victory Over the Darkness* will help readers grow in the strength and truth of their powerful identity in Jesus Christ.

Victory Over the Darkness Study Guide

✎ BETHANYHOUSE

Stay up-to-date on your favorite books and authors with our free e-newsletters. Sign up today at bethanyhouse.com.

Find us on Facebook. facebook.com/BHPnonfiction

Follow us on Twitter. @bethany_house